# CHARLOTTE'S WEB

Written by E.B. White

## Teacher Guide

www.MemoriaPress.com

CHARLOTTE'S WEB
Written by E.B. White

TEACHER GUIDE
Contributing Editors: Leigh Lowe, Brenda Janke, Anne Parry, Brittany Mann

ISBN 978-1-61538-048-0



Cover illustration by Starr Steinbach

# Contents

## PREPARING TO READ:

### REVIEW

- Orally review any previous vocabulary.
- Review the plot of the book as read so far.
- Periodically review the concepts of character, setting, and plot.

### STUDY GUIDE PREVIEW

- Reading Notes:
  - Read aloud together
  - This section gives the student key characters, places, terms that are relevant to a particular time period, etc.
- Vocabulary:
  - Read aloud together so that students will recognize words when they come across them in their reading.
- Comprehension Questions:
  - Read through these questions with students to encourage purposeful reading.

## READING:

- Student reads the chapter (or selection of the chapter for that lesson) independently or to the teacher (for younger students).
- For younger students, you can alternate between teacher-read and student-read passages. Model good reading skills. Encourage students to read expressively and smoothly. Teacher may occasionally take oral reading grades.
- While reading, mark each vocabulary word as you come across it.
- Have students take note in their study guide margin of pages where a comprehension question is answered.

## AFTER READING:

### VOCABULARY

- Look at each word within the context that it is used, and help your student come up with the best synonym that defines the word. (Make sure it is a synonym the student knows the meaning of.)
- Record the word's meaning in the students' study guides. (Use students' knowledge of Latin and other vocabulary to decipher meanings.)

### COMPREHENSION QUESTIONS

- Older students can answer these questions independently, but younger students (2nd-4th) need to answer the questions orally, form a good sentence, and then write it down, using correct punctuation, capitalization, and spelling. (You may want to write the sentence down for the younger student after forming it orally, and then let the student copy it perfectly.)
- It is not necessary to write the answer to every question. Some may be better answered orally.
- Answering questions and composing answers is a valuable learning activity. Questions require students to think; writing a concise answer is a good composition exercise.

### QUOTATIONS AND DISCUSSION QUESTIONS

- Use the Quotations and Discussion Questions section of each lesson as a guide to your oral discussion of the key concepts in the chapter that may not be covered in the comprehension questions.
- These talking points can take your oral discussion to a higher level than covered in the students' written work. Use this time as an opportunity to introduce higher-level thinking. You can introduce concepts the students may not be mature enough to fully understand yet but that would be beneficial for them to begin thinking about.
- A key to the Discussion Questions is in the back of the Teacher Guide.

### ENRICHMENT

- The Enrichment activities include composition, copywork, dictation, research, mapping, drawing, poetry work, literary terms, and more.
- This section has a variety of activities in it, but the most valuable activity is composition. Your student should complete at least one composition assignment each week. Proof student's work and have student copy composition until grammatically perfect. Insist on clear, concise writing. For younger students, start with 2-3 sentences, and do the assignment together. The student can form good sentences orally as you write them down, and then the student copies them.
- These activities can be completed as time and interest allow. Do not feel you need to complete all of these activities. Choose the ones that you feel are the best use of your students' time.

### UNIT REVIEW AND TESTS

- There is a unit review and a quiz or test following every few lessons (varies by individual guide).
- On the weeks that have these reviews and tests, you may want to do the review early in the week, and then drill it orally a couple of times before giving the test at the end of the week.
- A final comprehensive test is also included.

## Reading Notes

| | |
|---|---|
| **plaster** | a paste applied to walls which hardens as it dries |
| **roller towel** | a long, continuous towel sewed together and hung on a roller; it can be washed and reused |
| **dagger** | a short sword-like weapon |
| **specimen** | an example |

## Vocabulary

1. one of the pigs is a **runt**. smallest of the litter
2. I know more about raising a **litter** of pigs than you do. animal siblings born at the same time
3. This is the most terrible case of **injustice** I ever heard of. unfairness
4. Saved from an **untimely** death. occurring too soon
5. No, I only **distribute** pigs to early risers. to deliver, give out

## Comprehension Questions

1. Name each Arable family member, including the children's ages.

   The Arable family includes Father, Mother, Fern (age 8), and Avery (age 10).

2. How does Fern convince her father not to kill the runt? What is her reasoning?

   Fern tells her father that killing the runt is an unjust act. "The pig couldn't help being born small …"

3. What is the first thing Fern teaches her pig?

   Fern first teaches her pig to take milk from a bottle.

4. What does Fern name her pig? Why does she choose that name?

   Fern names her pig Wilbur because it is "the most beautiful name she could think of."

5. Why does Fern say "Wilbur" instead of answering her teacher's questions about Pennsylvania's capital? She is daydreaming about her pig and not paying attention.

## Quotations

*"But it's unfair," cried Fern. "The pig couldn't help being born small, could it? If* I *had been very small at birth, would you have killed* me*?" Mr. Arable smiled. "Certainly not," he said, looking down at his daughter with love. "But this is different. A little girl is one thing, a little runty pig is another."*

*Fern couldn't take her eyes off the tiny pig. "Oh," she whispered. "Oh,* look *at him! He's absolutely perfect."*

## Discussion Questions

1. *What does the word "arable" mean? From what Latin word does "arable" come? Why is it a good name for a farm family?
2. Study the pictures on pages 5 and 6. How has the illustrator contrasted Avery and Fern?
3. Reread Fern's objection to the runt's death and Mr. Arable's reply in the first quote above. In what way is a pig different than a little girl? Who do you agree with, and why?

   * Discussion questions that have a * are NECESSARY to discuss with students, as they may appear on a test and are generally important in understanding the full flavor of the story.

## Enrichment

**Focus Passage:** Copy the 2nd and 3rd paragraphs from page 5 (beginning with "Can I have a pig ..." and ending with "Let's eat!"

____________________________________________________________________________

____________________________________________________________________________

____________________________________________________________________________

____________________________________________________________________________

____________________________________________________________________________

____________________________________________________________________________

____________________________________________________________________________

____________________________________________________________________________

What is Mr. Arable subtly trying to communicate to Avery through his response?________________

He is telling Avery that he thinks he (Avery) sleeps too long and should be in the habit of getting up earlier.

## Reading Notes

| | |
|---|---|
| **apple-blossom time** | springtime |
| **enchanted** | fascinated |
| **manure** | animal excrement |
| **cellar** | a room beneath the barn |

## Vocabulary

1. He would stand and **gaze** up at her with adoring eyes. to look at steadily
2. Fern **peered** through the door. peeked
3. It **relieved** her mind to know that her baby would sleep covered up comforted
4. he would stand and watch the bus until it **vanished** around a turn. disappeared
5. When she **waded** into the brook, Wilbur waded in with her. walked in or through shallow water

## Comprehension Questions

1. How does Wilbur keep himself warm on cold nights?

   Wilbur keeps himself warm by burrowing into the straw.

2. Describe some of the ways Fern pampers Wilbur.

   Fern takes Wilbur for rides in her doll carriage and lets him wade in the mud while she swims. She cuddles him while feeding him warm milk from a bottle. She allows him the freedom to follow her all around the farm.

3. How does Fern feel about Wilbur? How does Wilbur feel about Fern?

   Fern loves Wilbur more than anything, and Wilbur adores Fern.

4. Who buys Wilbur? For how much?

   Uncle Homer Zuckerman buys Wilbur for six dollars.

## Quotations

*Fern loved Wilbur more than anything. She loved to stroke him, to feed him, to put him to bed. Every morning, as soon as she got up, she warmed his milk, tied his bib on, and held the bottle for him….Wilbur loved his milk, and he was never happier than when Fern was warming up a bottle for him. He would stand and gaze up at her with adoring eyes.*

*"He's got to go, Fern," he said. "You have had your fun raising a baby pig, but Wilbur is not a baby any longer and he has got to be sold."*

Who said this? Fern's father

## Discussion Questions

1. Since straw is not a main source of food, what is it used for on a farm?
2. Why is Fern's father able to predict what Wilbur will do to stay warm in his wooden box?
3. Why does Wilbur enjoy playing in the mud that is "delightfully sticky and oozy"?
4. *What reasons does Father give for insisting that Fern sell Wilbur?

## Enrichment

**Order and Describe:** List Wilbur's first three homes in their correct order. Then, below each one, list vivid words that describe it.

| 1. box in the kitchen | 2. box in the woodshed | 3. crate under apple tree |
|---|---|---|
| warm | larger | soft |
| cozy | lonely | most freedom |
| exciting | warm | warm |
| noisy | more freedom | interesting |
| busy | | calm/tranquil |
| | | |
| | | |
| | | |

## Reading Notes

| | |
|---|---|
| **grindstones, pitch forks, monkey wrenches, scythes** | tools used for sharpening, adjusting, and cutting |
| **rooting** | to dig up |
| **slops** | watery food |
| **hullabaloo** | a clamorous noise |

## Vocabulary

1. It smelled of the **perspiration** of tired horses ______ sweat
2. The cocker spaniel heard the **commotion** ______ noisy, confused activity
3. He's trying to **lure** you back into captivity-ivity. ______ to attract
4. He's trying to lure you back into **captivity**-ivity. ______ state of being held against your will
5. He's **appealing** to your stomach. ______ to attract through other means

## Comprehension Questions

1. What is a sheepfold? Why do you think the geese live with the sheep?

   A sheepfold is a pen in which sheep are kept. The geese are alert and protect the sheep by warning of danger approaching.

2. Who is the first animal Wilbur meets? How does she influence him?

   Wilbur first meets the goose. She encourages him to escape when he has the chance.

3. Why does Wilbur so willingly follow the advice of the goose at first?

   He is very bored and discouraged. He is young (naïve) and doesn't know what will happen as a result of his escape.

4. What is Wilbur's final opinion of his freedom and eventual recapture?

   He is glad to be recaptured. Freedom makes him nervous. He decides he is too young to be alone in the world.

## Quotations

*The barn was very large. It was very old. It smelled of hay and it smelled of manure. It smelled of the perspiration of tired horses and the wonderful sweet breath of patient cows. It often had a sort of peaceful smell—as though nothing bad could happen ever again in the world.*

*"I'm really too young to go out into the world alone," he thought as he lay down.*

Who said this? Wilbur On what occasion? after his escape and recapture

## Discussion Questions

1. Describe the barn; how it looks, what it contains, and how it feels.
2. *List the animals living in the barn. Describe the homes of each.
3. *Explain the goose's warning: "He's appealing to your stomach."
4. What causes Wilbur to change his mind about being free? What does he long for?

## Enrichment

**Focus Passage:** Copy the first full paragraph on page 14 (beginning with "Wilbur's new home …"). Spelling, punctuation, and capitalization should be perfect.

## Reading Notes

**hominy** dried corn
**provender** hay or oats used for livestock feed
**flibbertigibbet** a silly, scatterbrained person

## Vocabulary

1. I am a **glutton** but not a merrymaker. one who habitually overeats
2. And Templeton, the rat, crept **stealthily** along the wall sneakily
3. Usually he … was **abroad** only after dark. traveling far and wide
4. **dejected** and hungry, he threw himself down in the manure disappointed; discouraged
5. He didn't know whether he could **endure** the awful loneliness to bear, tolerate

## Comprehension Questions

1. Describe the appearance, personality, and attitude of Templeton.

   Templeton has whiskers and a sharp nose. He is crafty, sneaky, a loner, self-serving, greedy, secretive, and clever.

2. What does Wilbur do to try to cure his loneliness?

   He asks the other animals to play with him. He tries to make a friend.

3. How do the goose, Templeton, and the lamb react to Wilbur's request?

   They all give excuses and refuse to play with him.

4. Why does Wilbur declare the day the "worst of his life"?

   Wilbur is lonely and no one will play with him. His plans for the day are ruined because the rain keeps him from going outdoors.

5. What is Wilbur's pleasant surprise at the end of the day?

   He hears a voice speaking to him out of the darkness, offering him friendship.

## Quotations

*Wilbur didn't want food, he wanted love. He wanted a friend—someone who would play with him.*

*"I prefer to spend my time eating, gnawing, spying, and hiding. I am a glutton but not a merrymaker."*

Who said this? Templeton To whom? Wilbur

## Discussion Questions

1. *Which of the illustrations in Chapter 4 shows Wilbur at his saddest? How can you tell?
2. Who says, "Pigs mean less than nothing to me"? How does Wilbur respond to this statement?
3. In the second quote above, what does Templeton mean by "I am a glutton but not a merrymaker"?
4. What does Lurvy do to try to make Wilbur feel better? Why?

## Enrichment

**Composition:** Wilbur experienced a very disappointing and lonely day. He was not able to accomplish any of his plans for the day. Have you ever had a day like Wilbur's?

Directions: Write a paragraph (3-5 sentences) explaining your day. Use the following questions to guide your composition: What were your plans? How did they change? How did you feel? (Don't forget to indent your paragraph!)

## Reading Notes

**Charlotte *A. Cavatica*** a reference to a barn spider's scientific name, *Araneaus cavaticus*
**inheritance** a genetic characteristic passed from parent to offspring
**"by my wits"** by cleverness

## Vocabulary

1. I didn't mean to be **objectionable**. offensive, unpleasant
2. He lay down **meekly** in the manure humbly
3. A fly … **blundered** into the lower part of Charlotte's web moved carelessly, clumsily
4. and although he **detested** flies, he was sorry for this one. strongly disliked
5. Wilbur was **merely** suffering the doubts and fears only; simply

## Comprehension Questions

1. What word does Charlotte use to greet Wilbur? What Latin root means "greetings"? What is the opening of a friendly letter called? Charlotte greets Wilbur with "Salutations!" The Latin root is "salut-". The opening of a letter is called the "salutation."

2. How does the author describe Charlotte? How does Charlotte describe herself? The author describes Charlotte as a large, gray spider, about the size of a gumdrop. Charlotte describes herself as pretty, not very flashy, and near-sighted.

3. What does Charlotte do for a "living"? How does she capture prey? Charlotte is a "trapper." She builds webs and traps insects. She traps and eats insects by rolling and wrapping them in silk jets when they get stuck in her web. She then puts them to sleep (anesthetizes them) until she is ready to eat them.

4. How does Charlotte defend herself and convince Wilbur that webs are a good thing? She claims she has to eat and no one brings her food. Also, too many insects would destroy the earth.

## Quotations

*"Well," he thought, "I've got a new friend, all right. But what a gamble friendship is!"*

Who said this? Wilbur On what occasion? after meeting Charlotte

*Wilbur was merely suffering the doubts and fears that often go with finding a new friend. In good time he was to discover that he was mistaken about Charlotte. Underneath her rather bold and cruel exterior, she had a kind heart, and she was to prove loyal and true to the very end.*

## Discussion Questions

1. Before Charlotte greets him, Wilbur is impatient, embarrassed, and humble. Describe how Wilbur demonstrates these qualities toward the beginning of the chapter.
2. Describe in detail Charlotte's process for obtaining food.
3. Contrast how Charlotte obtains her food compared to how Wilbur receives his. What does this say about Charlotte?
4. *Explain Wilbur's statement, "... what a gamble friendship is!" in the first quote above.

## Enrichment

**Dialogue** is back-and-forth conversational exchange. Each time a new character begins speaking, there is a new set of quotation marks, and a new paragraph begins with indentation.

Directions: Copy the dialogue between Charlotte and Wilbur from page 37 (beginning with "'My name,' said the spider ..." and ending with "... as clearly as you can see me." Spelling, punctuation, and capitalization should be perfect.

## Reading Notes

| | |
|---|---|
| **swathes** | long, narrow rows of cut grass or grain |
| **jubilee** | celebration |
| **Fridgidaire** | a brand of refrigerator |
| **dud** | a failure |

## Vocabulary

1. Then the hay would be **hoisted** lifted, pulled up by a device
2. Sweet, sweet, sweet **interlude** a short break between two larger segments of music
3. after four weeks of **unremitting** effort and patience constant; neverending
4. The rat had no morals … no **scruples** … no anything. conscience; restraint
5. The rat had no morals … no **compunctions** … no anything. uneasiness caused by guilt; remorse
6. He pushed … till he succeeded in rolling it to his **lair**. den

## Comprehension Questions

1. Describe early summer days on the farm.

   Flowers and trees are blossoming. The days are warm. Farmers are harvesting the fields.

2. Where is Fern in this chapter? How do the animals treat her?

   She visits the barn almost every day. The animals treat her as an equal.

3. What is the important event that happens in the barn cellar? Who announces it?

   Charlotte makes the announcement that the goslings have hatched.

4. Where does Templeton put the "dud" goose egg?

   He rolls it to his den (lair) under the trough.

## Quotations

*The rat had no morals, no conscience, no scruples, no consideration, no decency, no milk of rodent kindness, no compunctions, no higher feeling, no friendliness, no anything. He would kill a gosling if he could get away with it—the goose knew that. Everybody knew it.*

*"But, my friends, if that ancient egg ever breaks, this barn will be untenable."*

What does "untenable" mean? unable to be lived in

## Discussion Questions

1. List four birds mentioned in the chapter. Describe each bird's song.
2. Explain the statement, "A rotten egg is a regular stink bomb."

## Enrichment

**Characterization:** Using what you know about Templeton from this chapter and previous ones, fill in the characterization chart below. Use specific examples from the book and include the page number of where the example was found.

| Ways Templeton's character is revealed | Example | What you learn about Templeton from this example |
|---|---|---|
| Templeton's speech | "I won't break it." "I know what I'm doing. I handle stuff like this all the time." p. 47 | Templeton is cocky, overly confident, and wants to show he is self-sufficient. |
| Templeton's appearance | beady eyes p. 45<br>sharp nose p. 30 | He looks suspicious. |
| How other characters feel about Templeton and react to him | "Everyone watched him, for he was not well liked, not trusted." p. 45<br>"The rat had no morals …" p. 46 | The animals do not trust Templeton and good reasons not to since he has no conscience. They know what he is really like. |
| Templeton's actions | "He glanced at Fern, then crept cautiously toward the goose …" p. 45<br>"Templeton was a crafty rat …" p. 30<br>He ate Wilbur's breakfast p. 30 | sneaky<br>smart, cunning<br>selfish, resourceful |

## Reading Notes

**victim** someone who is harmed by another
**anaesthetic** pain killer
**conspiracy** secret plan to do harm

## Vocabulary

1. Her **campaign** against insects seemed sensible and useful. intense activity for a specific purpose
2. Her campaign against insects seemed **sensible** and useful. wise
3. Flies spent their time **pestering** others. bothering
4. The sheep **loathed** them. strongly disliked
5. I can't stand **hysterics**. exaggerated, uncontrolled emotions

## Comprehension Questions

1. What does Charlotte do that Wilbur describes as "real thoughtful"?

   She gives her prey an anaesthetic before drinking their blood.

2. What bad news is spreading in the barnyard? Who passes it on to Wilbur?

   The old sheep tells Wilbur that he is going to be killed at Christmastime.

3. Contrast Wilbur's and Charlotte's reactions to the bad news.

   Wilbur becomes worried and frantic. Charlotte stays calm yet agrees that it is a dirty trick.

4. What promise does Charlotte make?

   She promises to save Wilbur from death.

5. What does Charlotte tell Wilbur to do? Why?

   She tells Wilbur to stop crying because she can't stand hysterics.

## Quotations

*Wilbur liked Charlotte better and better each day. Her campaign against insects seemed sensible and useful.*

*Wilbur burst into tears. "I don't* ***want*** *to die," he moaned. "I want to stay alive, right here in my comfortable manure pile with all my friends. I want to breathe the beautiful air and lie in the beautiful sun."*

## Discussion Questions

1. *Think about the first quote above and the first few paragraphs of the chapter. How has Wilbur's opinion of Charlotte's activities changed?
2. *Reread the second quote above. How has Wilbur's outlook on life been altered since his earlier days on the farm?

## Enrichment

**Quotation Review:** How good is your memory? Supply the name of the speaker for each quotation below.

1. "But it's unfair … The pig couldn't help being born small, could it?" Fern
2. "I only distribute pigs to early risers." Mr. Arable
3. "Get around behind him, Lurvy … and drive him toward the barn!" Mr. Zuckerman
4. "No-no-no … It's the old pail trick, Wilbur. Don't fall for it!" goose
5. "Pigs mean less than nothing to me." lamb
6. "I am a glutton but not a merrymaker." Templeton
7. "I'll be a friend to you. I've watched you all day and I like you." Charlotte
8. "… they're fattening you up because they're going to kill you …" old sheep
9. "Stop! … I don't want to die! Save me, somebody!" Wilbur
10. "… Stop your crying! I can't stand hysterics." Charlotte

# Elements of Literature

Write sentences about the story.

## Character

**Character** means who is in the story.

1. Write one declarative sentence describing Wilbur. Include his age and personality. ____________

   Answers will vary.

2. Write one interrogative sentence (question) about another character in the story. Include words that describe this character's appearance and personality. ____________

   Answers will vary.

## Setting

**Setting** means the time and place in which the story happens.

1. Write one exclamatory sentence about the Arable farm. ____________

   Answers will vary.

2. Write one descriptive sentence about Mr. Zuckerman's barn. Be sure to include strong imagery (sights, sounds, smells) in your sentence. ____________

   Answers will vary.

## Plot

**Plot** means action or what happens in the story.

Directions: Sequence the events in order. Then, copy them in order onto the following page. Each event should be written below a separate box. Finally, illustrate each event in the box.

**Events:**

__4__ Charlotte became Wilbur's friend.

__2__ Wilbur escaped from his pen.

__6__ Wilbur learned he would be killed at Christmastime.

__1__ Fern saved and cared for Wilbur.

__5__ Templeton requested the rotten goose egg.

__3__ Wilbur was lonely and bored.

# Storyboard

1

Fern saved and cared for Wilbur.

2

Wilbur escaped from his pen.

3

Wilbur was lonely and bored.

4

Charlotte became Wilbur's friend.

5

Templeton requested the rotten goose egg.

6

Wilbur learned he would be killed at Christmastime.

# Vocabulary

Write the letter of the vocabulary word on the line in front of its definition.

| | | |
|---|---|---|
| 1. __h__ | smallest of the litter | a. blundered |
| 2. __b__ | unfairness | b. injustice |
| 3. __m__ | to deliver; give out | c. commotion |
| 4. __s__ | to look at steadily | d. meekly |
| 5. __j__ | disappeared | e. waded |
| 6. __e__ | walked in shallow water | f. endure |
| 7. __o__ | state of being held against your will | g. hysterics |
| 8. __c__ | noisy, confused activity | h. runt |
| 9. __t__ | to attract through other means | i. loathed |
| 10. __q__ | one who habitually overeats | j. vanished |
| 11. __f__ | to bear, tolerate | k. dejected |
| 12. __k__ | disappointed; discouraged | l. merely |
| 13. __d__ | humbly | m. distribute |
| 14. __l__ | only; simply | n. hoisted |
| 15. __a__ | moved carelessly | o. captivity |
| 16. __n__ | lifted; pulled up by a device | p. lair |
| 17. __p__ | den | q. glutton |
| 18. __r__ | constant; neverending | r. unremitting |
| 19. __g__ | exaggerated, uncontrolled emotions | s. gaze |
| 20. __i__ | strongly disliked | t. appealing |

# Short Answer

Answer the following questions in complete sentences.

1. What does the word "arable" mean? Why is it a good name for a farm family?

   "Arable" means land suitable for farming. It is a good name because the Arables are farmers.

2. What reasons does Father give for insisting that Fern sell Wilbur?

   Wilbur is beginning to eat more food. Mr. Arable is not willing to provide food for him any longer because the cost of the food would be more than the price he could get selling him later. Mr. Arable has already sold Wilbur's siblings.

3. What important event, announced by Charlotte, happens in the barn cellar?

   Charlotte makes the announcement that the goslings have hatched.

4. Explain Wilbur's statement, "… what a gamble friendship is!"

   When you first befriend someone, you don't really know them well and the friendship may or may not work out. You need to be willing to get to know the other person instead of dismissing them because you have differences.

5. What promise does Charlotte make to Wilbur?

   Charlotte promises to save Wilbur from death.

# Reading Notes

**goslings** (pronounced "goz-lings") baby geese

**Sunday School** a class for religious instruction that meets on Sundays

# Vocabulary

1. gazing at her daughter with a **queer**, worried look. strange
2. She's **terribly** clever. extremely
3. "Does he really?" said Mrs. Arable, rather **vaguely**. without clear thought
4. I haven't the **faintest** idea, least
5. every one of us … will be **gratified** to learn pleased; satisfied
6. Did you hear the way she **rambled** on about the animals …? talked incessantly

# Comprehension Questions

1. Why is Mrs. Arable worried about Fern?

   Fern claims that she understands what the animals are saying.

2. How does Mr. Arable respond to Mrs. Arable's concern?

   Mr. Arable says that maybe animals do talk, and that Fern has a good imagination.

3. What does Mrs. Arable plan to do to ease her mind about Fern?

   Mrs. Arable plans to talk to Dr. Dorian about Fern's strange behavior.

4. Fern often sits quietly on a stool in the barn. After reading this chapter, what do you now know she has been doing while in the barn?

   Fern has been listening and understanding the animals' conversation.

## Quotations

*"She's Wilbur's best friend. She's terribly clever."*

Who said this? Fern ______ To whom? her mother ______

*Mr. Arable grinned. "Maybe our ears aren't as sharp as Fern's," he said.*

## Discussion Questions

1. What is your opinion about talking animals?

## Enrichment

**Focus Passage:** Copy the third and fourth full paragraphs from page 54 (beginning with "I worry about Fern …" and ending with "… all sorts of things.")

**Notice**: There are two separate paragraphs that need to be indented. Be careful to copy all quotation marks accurately. Spelling, punctuation, and capitalization should be perfect.

## Reading Notes

| | |
|---|---|
| **hitches** | easily loosened knots that attach a rope to an object |
| **sedentary** | accustomed to sitting or to taking little exercise |
| **truffles** | edible fungi; grow near the roots of trees |
| **troupe** | a group of musicians |

## Vocabulary

1. He glanced **hastily** behind to see if a piece of rope was following him quickly
2. Anything to **oblige**. to help
3. And **summoning** all his strength, he threw himself into the air gathering; calling up
4. In a forest looking for … **delectable** roots delicious; tasty
5. But don't fail to let me know … no matter how **slight**. small

## Comprehension Questions

1. List the sections of Charlotte's legs. What interesting attributes do her legs have?

   coxa, trochanter, femur, patella, tibia, metatarsus, tarsus

   Her legs are hairy, strong, and agile.

2. How does Wilbur try to imitate Charlotte? Why does he fail?

   Wilbur tries to spin a web of his own, but he doesn't have spinnerets or "know-how."

3. In what ways does Charlotte think her webs are better than human "webs" (i.e., bridges)?

   Her webs can be made in one evening instead of in eight years. She can sit still and wait for food to come to her instead of rushing around like humans do. Her webs are more practical for catching prey.

4. What instructions does Charlotte give Wilbur to help carry out "the plan"?

   She tells him to get plenty of sleep, slow down, stop worrying, eat his food, gain weight, stay well, keep fit, and not to lose his nerve.

## Quotations

*While the rat and the spider and the little girl watched, Wilbur climbed again to the top of the manure pile, full of energy and hope.*

*"I want you to get plenty of sleep, and stop worrying. Never hurry and never worry! Chew your food thoroughly and eat every bit of it, except you must leave just enough for Templeton. Gain weight and stay well—that's the way you can help."*

Who said this? Charlotte To whom? Wilbur

## Discussion Questions

1. In this chapter, Wilbur tries several times to accomplish something that he was not made to do. How can we discover our own unique gifts and talents? How can we encourage our friends and family to do the same?
2. What observations does Charlotte make about people in this chapter? Do you think she is correct in her assumptions?

## Enrichment

**Studying Details:** Using the diagram of a spider in the Appendix as a reference, draw a detailed diagram of Charlotte below.

Label the seven parts of her legs and her spinnerets.

Complete your diagram by coloring it.

## Reading Notes

| | |
|---|---|
| **crisis** | a terrible event |
| **gabbled** | to speak rapidly and in a way that is difficult to understand |
| **astride** | to sit or stand with one leg on each side of an object |

## Vocabulary

1. people are very **gullible**. easily deceived
2. Then you **straddled** the knot, so that it acted as a seat. stand with one leg on each side
3. Templeton … **scuttled** away into the barn. scurried
4. "It pays to save things," he said in his **surly** voice. unfriendly; bad-tempered
5. After a while she **bestirred** herself. roused; moved
6. She worked slowly … while the other creatures **drowsed**. napped

## Comprehension Questions

1. On what attribute does Charlotte rely to help her solve problems? Give examples.
   Charlotte relies on patience to solve problems. She waits patiently for flies to land in her web and she sits quietly and thoughtfully as she works out solutions to problems.
2. What idea comes to Charlotte to save Wilbur's life? Why does she think it will work?
   Charlotte's idea is to play a trick on Zuckerman. She thinks it will work because people are not as smart as insects. They are gullible.
3. What event stirs the barn animals and prevents a catastrophe? What catastrophe is prevented?
   As he is trying to capture Charlotte, Avery falls and breaks Templeton's rotten goose egg. The stench is so bad he gives up and runs from the barn, distracting Avery from capturing and harming Charlotte.
4. At the end of the chapter, why does Wilbur leave a whole noodle instead of half a noodle for Templeton? He remembers that the rat had been useful in saving Charlotte's life and Charlotte was trying to save his own life.

## Quotations

*"Why, how perfectly simple!" she said to herself. "The way to save Wilbur's life is to play a trick on Zuckerman. If I can fool a bug," thought Charlotte, "I can surely fool a man. People are not as smart as bugs."*

*The spider, however, stayed wide awake, gazing affectionately at him and making plans for his future. Summer was half gone. She knew she didn't have much time.*

## Discussion Questions

1. Reread the second quote above. Has Wilbur done anything to earn or deserve Charlotte's affection? What does that say about the nature of friendship?
2. In what ways are Templeton, the goose, and Lurvy "accidental" heroes?
3. Describe the highlights of Fern's and Avery's day at the Zuckerman farm.

## Enrichment

**Dictation:** Listen carefully as your teacher reads to you from page 72 (beginning with "Fern was crying …" through "… a narrow escape."). During the reading, write down what you hear. Then go back and make any necessary corrections in spelling, punctuation, or capitalization. When you are finished, compare your paragraph to the book and circle any errors.

Note for instructor: Students should have their books closed during dictation. The passage should be read aloud only two times.

The first time the students write as much as they can, skipping a space if they miss a word. The second time students should fill in any blank spaces they may have and check for accuracy. Allow some time for them to make corrections in spelling, etc. They then should check their own work, using the passage in the book, circling or correcting any errors.

DICTATE: "Fern was crying. She held her nose and ran toward the house. Avery ran after her, holding his nose. Charlotte felt greatly relieved to see him go. It had been a narrow escape."

## Reading Notes

| | |
|---|---|
| **spang** | directly |
| **Studebaker, Packard, De Soto** | types of cars; now antiques |
| **buckboard** | a four-wheeled wagon drawn by a horse or other large animal |

## Vocabulary

1. Charlotte, sleepy after her night's **exertions**, smiled ____physical efforts; work____
2. Instead, he walked **solemnly** back up to the house ____seriously____
3. A look of complete **bewilderment** came over Mrs. Zuckerman's face. ____confusion____
4. She's a rather queer child—full of **notions**. ____ideas____
5. his **principal** farm duty was to feed the pig ____main; primary____

## Comprehension Questions

1. Describe the beauty of the web. Who was the first person to discover it?

   (refer to the first two paragraphs of the chapter) The web glistened with beads of water along its thin strands. It had a pattern like a delicate veil. Lurvy discovered it first.

2. Charlotte's plan is finally unveiled. Describe it, and explain how it helps Wilbur.

   She writes "Some pig" in her web to draw attention to Wilbur's goodness. Everyone pays attention to Wilbur and begins to believe he is a very special pig.

3. How does Mrs. Zuckerman's view of the miracle differ from everyone else's?

   She recognizes that it is the spider who is special because she is capable of spelling and writing.

4. What are specific ways the web affects life on the Zuckerman farm?

   People come to see Wilbur and the web, Mr. Zuckerman neglects his farm work and wears good clothes all the time. Mrs. Zuckerman prepares special meals for Wilbur. Lurvy shaves and gets a haircut.

## Quotations

*Secrets are hard to keep. Long before Sunday came, the news spread all over the county. Everybody knew that a sign had appeared in a spider's web on the Zuckerman place. Everybody knew that the Zuckermans had a wondrous pig.*

*Mr. Zuckerman ordered Lurvy to increase Wilbur's feedings from three meals a day to four meals a day.*

## Discussion Questions

1. In the previous chapter, Charlotte said that humans are gullible. Give examples of specific ways from this chapter that prove Charlotte was correct in her observation.
2. Why do the Zuckermans and Lurvy change their personal appearance and habits once Wilbur becomes famous?

## Enrichment

**Character Study:** Match each character to his or her reaction to Charlotte's web.

| Lurvy | Mr. Zuckerman | townspeople | Fern |
|---|---|---|---|
| minister | Mrs. Arable | Mrs. Zuckerman | |

1. Mr. Zuckerman "But we have received a sign … a miracle has happened on this farm."
2. minister "… this community has been visited by a wondrous animal."
3. Mrs. Arable was so shocked that she sent Avery to bed for punishment
4. Mrs. Zuckerman "It seems to me we have no ordinary *spider.*"
5. Lurvy dropped to his knees and uttered a short prayer
6. Fern was happy but felt the barn was not nearly as pleasant
7. townspeople came to stand hour after hour at Wilbur's pen, admiring him

## Reading Notes

**St. Vitus's Dance** a disorder characterized by jerky, uncontrollable movements
**baser instincts** needs or behaviors vital for survival

## Vocabulary

1. It's my idio-idio-**idiosyncrasy**. peculiar habit
2. Any suggestions for a new **slogan**? a phrase used in advertising to get attention
3. Wilbur's **destiny** and your **destiny** are closely linked. fate, future
4. Templeton's whiskers **quivered**. trembled
5. The meeting is now **adjourned**. officially ended

## Comprehension Questions

1. What does Charlotte want to discuss at the meeting? Who attends? Charlotte asks for suggestions for the next web message. The geese, sheep, Wilbur and (later) Templeton attend Charlotte's meeting.

2. What role does the old sheep suggest Templeton could play in the plan to save Wilbur? The old sheep suggests that Templeton could bring back magazine clippings from the dump as ideas for the web message.

3. Why is Charlotte worried about Templeton's involvement? Charlotte's concern is that he only looks out for himself and might not be trustworthy.

4. What argument does the old sheep use to get Templeton to agree to help? The sheep points out that saving Wilbur will mean Templeton will always have food, since Wilbur's leftovers are his main food source.

## Quotations

*"The message I wrote in my web, praising Wilbur, has been received. The Zuckermans have fallen for it, and so has everybody else. Zuckerman thinks Wilbur is an unusual pig, and therefore he won't want to kill him and eat him. I dare say my trick will work and Wilbur's life can be saved."*

Who said this? Charlotte On what occasion? at the meeting in the barn

*"You're terrific as far as* I'm *concerned," replied Charlotte, sweetly, "and that's what counts. You're my best friend, and* I *think you're sensational."*

## Discussion Questions

1. Reread the first quote above. Why is Charlotte so confident that her plan to save Wilbur will work?
2. *What is Wilbur's reaction to the new word? What does this show about his character?
3. Why are some words italicized in the last two paragraphs of the chapter?

## Enrichment

**Focus Passage:** Copy the second quote above. Pay close attention to quotation marks. (Ignore the italics.) Spelling, punctuation, and capitalization should be perfect.

## Reading Notes

| | |
|---|---|
| **orb** | a sphere or spherical object |
| **radial** | moving from the center to the outside of a circle (spokes) |
| **aeronaut** | a pilot or traveler in a hot air balloon |

## Vocabulary

1. Templeton was down there now, **rummaging** around. searching in an untidy manner
2. "There!" he said, **triumphantly**. victoriously
3. With New **Radiant** Action. glowing, sending out warmth
4. Wilbur went over backwards, **writhing** and twisting as he went. squirming
5. Tired from his **romp**, Wilbur lay down lively play; frolicking

## Comprehension Questions

1. Describe the types of thread Charlotte can produce. How is each used?

   Charlotte produces dry, tough thread for foundation lines and sticky threads for snare lines.

2. How does Charlotte entertain herself while weaving?

   Charlotte talks to herself and cheers herself on as she weaves.

3. How do the words in Charlotte's web continue to affect how Wilbur is treated?

   Mr. Zuckerman tells Lurvy to give Wilbur only clean, bright straw for his bedding. He has also decided to bring Wilbur to the county fair.

4. What two things does Charlotte do to help Wilbur go to sleep? How does this show her affectionate friendship toward Wilbur?

   Charlotte tells Wilbur stories about her cousins and sings him a lullaby even though she herself is tired. She sacrifices her own comfort for her friend.

## Quotations

*Everybody stood at the pigpen and stared at the web and read the word, over and over, while Wilbur, who really* felt *terrific, stood quietly swelling out his chest and swinging his snout from side to side.*

*"Just the wrong idea," replied Charlotte. "Couldn't be worse. We don't want Zuckerman to think Wilbur is crunchy. He might start thinking about crisp, crunchy bacon and tasty ham. That would put ideas into his head. We must advertise Wilbur's noble qualities, not his tastiness. Go get another word, please, Templeton!"*

## Discussion Questions

1. List some of the things Templeton finds in the dump.
2. Describe some of the amazing qualities and abilities of Charlotte's relatives.

## Enrichment

**Italics** are used to indicate titles of newspapers, books, or magazines. When copying italics, underline the words that are italicized. Italics can also be used to show emphasis. (Example: "… while Wilbur, who really *felt* terrific …")

Directions: Reread the first full paragraph on page 96 (beginning with "Terrific!" breathed …") Then copy it below. Pay close attention to the italicized title of the newspaper, and underline it in your paragraph. Spelling, punctuation, and capitalization should be perfect.

___________________________________________

___________________________________________

___________________________________________

___________________________________________

___________________________________________

___________________________________________

___________________________________________

___________________________________________

___________________________________________

___________________________________________

___________________________________________

## Reading Notes

| | |
|---|---|
| **fib** | small lie; to tell a small lie |
| **crochet** | needlework made by looping thread using a hooked needle |
| **doily** | a small decorative mat made of thread |

## Vocabulary

1. "Fern," said her mother **sternly**, "you must not invent things." seriously, firmly
2. she was beaten **mercilessly** over the head by the … fish without compassion
3. and is carried **aloft** on the wind. into the air
4. It is a very **sociable** place. friendly
5. an animal has spoken **civilly** to me politely
6. People are **incessant** talkers endless; continuous

## Comprehension Questions

1. Why is Mrs. Arable alarmed by her conversation with Fern?
   Mrs. Arable is worried that Fern is not "normal" because she thinks she can hear animals talk.
2. Describe Dr. Dorian. Dr. Dorian is old, bearded, and intelligent. He has an easygoing attitude about Fern and is not worried about her.
3. How old is Fern? What does Dr. Dorian think about Fern's love of animals and spending so much time in the barn? Fern is eight years old. Dr. Dorian thinks Fern's love for animals is healthy and he understands her desire to sit in a quiet barn.
4. What observations does Dr. Dorian make about people? What is his opinion about spider webs?
   He thinks that if people talked less, animals would talk more and that any spider web is a miracle.
5. What does Dr. Dorian suggest will, in time, get Fern's attention?
   He thinks Fern will eventually turn her attention from animals to boys.

## Quotations

*"Alone?" said Fern. "Alone? My best friends are in the barn cellar. It is a very sociable place. Not at all lonely."*

*"It is quite possible that an animal has spoken civilly to me and that I didn't catch the remark because I wasn't paying attention. Children pay better attention than grownups. If Fern says that the animals in Zuckerman's barn talk, I'm quite ready to believe her. Perhaps if people talked less, animals would talk more. People are incessant talkers—I can give you my word on that."*

Who said this? Dr. Dorian To whom? Mrs. Arable

## Discussion Questions

1. *Refer to the second quote above. How does Dr. Dorian explain the difference between the "miracle" of a spider web and the fact that Mrs. Arable can crochet a doily and knit a sock?
2. Contrast Mrs. Arable's and Dr. Dorian's attitudes about things they do not understand. Is there something you don't like because you don't understand it? How could you change your opinion?

## Enrichment

**Dialogue:** Recall that **dialogue** is back-and-forth conversational exchange, and that **quotation marks** are used to show a person's exact words.

Directions: Insert quotation marks where they are needed in the following sentences.

1. "Charlotte is the best storyteller I ever heard," said Fern.
2. "What kind of story did she tell?" asked Mrs. Arable.
3. "Well," began Fern, "she told us about her cousin who caught a fish in her web."
4. "Fern!" snapped her mother. "Stop it! Stop inventing these wild tales!"
5. "I'm not inventing," said Fern. "I'm just telling you the facts."
6. "It's about Fern," she explained. "Fern spends entirely too much time in the Zuckermans' barn."
7. "How enchanting!" he said. "It must be real nice and quiet down there."
8. "I suppose so," said Mrs. Arable. "I never looked at it that way before. Still, I don't understand it."
9. "None of us do," said Dr. Dorian, sighing. "I don't understand everything, and I don't let it worry me."
10. "Well," said Dr. Dorian, "I think she will always love animals."

## Reading Notes

**reputation** the characteristics or traits a person is known for
**twitch** a short, sudden pull or tug

## Vocabulary

1. the song of summer's ending, a sad, **monotonous** song. unchanging
2. Wilbur was **modest**; fame did not spoil him. humble
3. If he could **distinguish** himself at the Fair to earn recognition
4. "Oh, sure," said the spider. "I'm **versatile**." adaptable; can adjust easily
5. Charlotte … **moodily** watched it sway. gloomily

## Comprehension Questions

1. How does Wilbur try to live up to his reputation?
   He tries to be as much like the web words as he can.
2. How has Charlotte influenced Wilbur's attitude towards life?
   He usually feels happy and confident because Charlotte has given him hope for the future.
3. What does Wilbur do to act out the word "radiant"?
   He turns his head slightly, bats his long eyelashes, breathes deeply, and occasionally does a back flip.
4. What are Wilbur and Charlotte each looking forward to? How do these clash?
   Wilbur is looking forward to his trip to the fair, and Charlotte is looking forward to laying her eggs. The conflict is that Wilbur wants Charlotte to accompany him to the fair, but she needs to stay home and lay her eggs.
5. Why can't Charlotte delay her egg laying until after the fair?
   Egg laying is subject to nature's timing. Charlotte can't rearrange her family duties to suit the dates of the fair—not even for Wilbur.

## Quotations

*Some of Wilbur's friends in the barn worried for fear all this attention would go to his head and make him stuck up. But it never did. Wilbur was modest; fame did not spoil him.*

*In the daytime, Wilbur usually felt happy and confident. No pig ever had truer friends, and he realized that friendship is one of the most satisfying things in the world.*

## Discussion Questions

1. ***A Lesson in Friendship:** Reread the second quote above. Describe how the following characters showed true friendship to Wilbur: Charlotte, Fern, the goose, the old sheep.
2. Describe some of the changes the farm experiences as the transition from summer to autumn begins.
3. How does the book hint at some future event concerning Charlotte? Does it sound exciting or unpleasant?

## Enrichment

**Focus Passage:** Copy the second paragraph on page 114 (beginning with "The sheep heard the crickets …" through "… bright red with anxiety."). Spelling, punctuation, and capitalization should be perfect.

# Elements of Literature

Write sentences about the story.

## Character

**Character** means who is in the story.

1. Write one declarative sentence describing Charlotte. ______

   Answers will vary.

2. Write a declarative sentence about another character in the story. Include words that describe this character's appearance and personality. ______

   Answers will vary.

## Setting

**Setting** means the time and place in which the story happens.

1. Write two sentences describing the change of seasons in Chapter 15. ______

   Answers will vary.

## Plot

**Plot** means action or what happens in the story.

Directions: Sequence the events in order. Then, copy them in order onto the following page. Each event should be written below a separate box. Finally, illustrate each event in the box.

**Events:**

_3_ A "miracle" occurs in the barn.

_5_ Two new webs are spun.

_1_ Wilbur tries unsuccessfully to spin a web.

_4_ The animals hold a meeting.

_6_ Dr. Dorian gives Fern's mother good advice.

_2_ A rotten goose egg saves Charlotte's life.

# Storyboard

1

Wilbur tries unsuccessfully to spin a web.

2

A rotten goose egg saves Charlotte's life.

3

A "miracle" occurs in the barn.

4

The animals hold a meeting.

5

Two new webs are spun.

6

Dr. Dorian gives Fern's mother good advice.

# Vocabulary

Write the letter of the vocabulary word on the line in front of its definition.

| | | |
|---|---|---|
| 1. t | seriously; firmly | a. gullible |
| 2. l | pleased; satisfied | b. sociable |
| 3. r | unchanging | c. principal |
| 4. h | without clear thought | d. delectable |
| 5. i | into the air | e. quivered |
| 6. c | main; primary | f. bestirred |
| 7. s | physical efforts; work | g. writhing |
| 8. e | trembled | h. vaguely |
| 9. b | friendly | i. aloft |
| 10. g | squirming | j. summoning |
| 11. j | gathering; calling up | k. modest |
| 12. d | delicious; tasty | l. gratified |
| 13. k | humble | m. romp |
| 14. p | endless; continuous | n. versatile |
| 15. m | lively play; frolicking | o. adjourned |
| 16. a | easily deceived | p. incessant |
| 17. f | roused; moved | q. surly |
| 18. n | adaptable; can adjust easily | r. monotonous |
| 19. q | unfriendly; bad-tempered | s. exertions |
| 20. o | officially ended | t. sternly |

## Short Answer

Answer the following questions in complete sentences.

1. What plan does Charlotte come up with to save Wilbur's life? Why does she think it will work?

   Charlotte plans to play a trick on Zuckerman because people are not as smart as insects. They are gullible.

2. Name two specific ways in which the webs affect life on the Zuckerman farm.

   Possible answers: people come to see Wilbur and the web, Mr. Zuckerman neglects his farm work and wears good clothes, Mrs. Zuckerman prepares special meals for Wilbur, Lurvy shaves and gets a haircut.

3. What is Wilbur's reaction to the second word in the web ("terrific")? What does this show about his character?

   Wilbur blushes and says he is just an average pig. This reaction shows that he is humble.

4. As summer comes to an end, what are Wilbur and Charlotte each looking forward to?

   Wilbur is looking forward to the fair, and Charlotte is looking forward to laying her eggs. They conflict because Wilbur wants Charlotte with him at the fair, but she needs to stay on the farm.

5. Choose one of the following characters and describe how he/she shows friendship towards Wilbur: Charlotte, Fern, the goose, the old sheep.

   **Charlotte** stands up for Wilbur, and she sacrifices her time and energy to help him. **Fern** saves Wilbur's life and visits him. **The goose** is friendly and kind and tries to suggest words. **The old sheep** tells him the truth and convinces Templeton to help.

## Reading Notes

| | |
|---|---|
| **midway** | the area of a fair where the food, rides, and games are located |
| **loot** | stolen goods |
| **yarn** | an entertaining tale |
| **stowaway** | a secret traveler |
| **tailgate** | a door at the back of a vehicle that is lowered during loading and unloading |

## Vocabulary

1. you will find a **veritable** treasure of popcorn fragments ___ true ___
2. the conditions at a fair will **surpass** your wildest dreams. ___ to exceed; go beyond ___
3. Don't go without a **tussle**. ___ struggle ___
4. I don't want to be **pummeled** … **buffeted** … **biffed** ___ all three are synonyms for "beaten" ___
5. I don't want to be … **lacerated** ___ cut ___

## Comprehension Questions

1. What does Fern wear to the fair? Why?

   Fern wears her prettiest dress because she knows she will see boys at the fair.

2. What special treatment does Wilbur get before departing for the fair?

   Wilbur gets a buttermilk bath before going to the fair.

3. Why does Charlotte finally decide to go with Wilbur to the fair?

   She thinks Wilbur may need her. She is being a friend by putting his needs ahead of her own.

4. Why does the old sheep want to tempt Templeton to go to the fair? What delicious items does he tell the rat he will find? The old sheep knows that Templeton could be a help to Charlotte and Wilbur at the fair. The sheep promises the rat he will find popcorn, candied apples, popsicles, lollypops, tuna fish, and much more at the fair.

5. What advice does the old sheep give Wilbur before he is crated for the fair? Why?

   He tells Wilbur to struggle as the men try to put him in the crate, because it would look suspicious for a pig not to resist.

## Quotations

*"That's some pig!" said Mrs. Arable. "He's terrific," said Lurvy. "He's very radiant," said Fern, remembering the day he was born. "Well," said Mrs. Zuckerman, "he's clean, anyway. The buttermilk certainly helped."*

*Then, using all their strength, the men picked up the crate and heaved it aboard the truck. They did not know that under the straw was a rat, and inside a knothole was a big grey spider. They saw only a pig.*

## Discussion Questions

1. Describe the dreams of Fern, Avery, Mr. and Mrs. Zuckerman, and Lurvy the night before the fair.
2. *Reread the first quote above. How do the words in the web continue to influence people's thinking about Wilbur?
3. Authors often use repetition to emphasize a point in a story. In what way does the author use repetition in this chapter to make the story more interesting?

## Enrichment

**Literary Tools - Description:** A good author uses descriptive words to paint a verbal picture for the reader.

Directions: Reread the last paragraph on page 122 (beginning with "That's because you've ..." through "... a whole army of rats.").

A. Find, record, and discuss two or three descriptive phrases used by the author.

Answers will vary, and should come directly from the wording of the paragraph.

Examples: foul remains of peanut butter sandwiches, veritable treasure of popcorn fragments,

partially gnawed ice cream cones, etc.

B. Add your own descriptive words to these examples from the paragraph.

hard-boiled eggs: Answers will vary.

cracker crumbs: ______

popsicles: ______

C. Think of another item Templeton may have found at the fair. Write your own descriptive phrase, being sure to paint a vivid mental picture for the reader.

Answers will vary.

## Reading Notes

**blatting** bleating
**deep freeze** a large freezer that resembles a chest

## Vocabulary

1. She **ascended** slowly and returned to Wilbur's pen. moved upward
2. She looked rather swollen and she seemed **listless**. tired, no energy
3. "Perhaps," she said, **wearily**. tiredly
4. Wilbur heard several people make **favorable** remarks positive, complimentary
5. The day grew **fiercely** hot. excessively

## Comprehension Questions

1. Describe the sights, sounds, and smells of the fair.

   The fair is filled with all sorts of animal noises, music, the smells of food and dust, and the sight of the Ferris wheel and balloons floating in the sky.

2. What privileges do Mr. and Mrs. Arable grant Fern and Avery at the fair?

   Fern and Avery are given money to spend and are allowed to go to the midway alone.

3. Name Wilbur's main competitor. Why does Charlotte dislike him?

   Wilbur's competitor is named Uncle. Charlotte finds him dirty, unpleasant in personality, noisy, and the teller of weak jokes.

4. What changes does Charlotte begin to notice in herself while at the fair?

   Charlotte feels a lack of energy and is tired all the time.

## Quotations

*The children grabbed each other by the hand and danced off in the direction of the merry-go-round, toward the wonderful music and the wonderful adventure and the wonderful excitement, into the wonderful midway where there would be no parents to guard them and guide them and where they could be happy and free and do as they pleased.*

*Charlotte, watching her chance, scrambled out of the crate and climbed a post to the under side of the roof. Nobody noticed her.*

## Discussion Questions

1. *Reread the second quote above, focusing on the last sentence. Why do you think Charlotte doesn't want to be noticed? What does she prefer?
2. *What signs are there of Wilbur becoming a better friend towards Charlotte?
3. Think back to the dreams in the beginning of Chapter 16. Did any of them come true in this chapter? Predict the outcome of Mr. Zuckerman's dream.

## Enrichment

**Focus Passage - Dialogue:** Recall that **dialogue** is used to show a character's exact words. Each time a different character begins to speak, a new paragraph is begun and indented.

Directions: Copy the paragraphs of dialogue on page 131 (beginning with "And if you go …" through "… cried Mrs. Zuckerman."). Spelling, punctuation, and capitalization should be perfect.

___

___

___

___

___

___

___

___

___

## Reading Notes

**beano booth** a forerunner of the game Bingo, using beans as markers
**schemer** a planner of a secret plot
**grandstand** the main seating area of a stadium

## Vocabulary

1. Templeton's **keen** nose detected many fine smells in the air. sharp, highly developed
2. Templeton's keen nose **detected** many fine smells in the air. identified
3. "Well, I hope you're satisfied," **sneered** the rat. spoke in a scornful or contemptuous manner
4. He **vanished** into the shadows. disappeared
5. I will show you my **masterpiece**. greatest work

## Comprehension Questions

1. What does Charlotte say about the web she is preparing?

   She says it will be her last web so she wants an especially fitting word to use in it.

2. What is the last word Charlotte weaves into her web? Why is it a perfect choice?

   Humble. Humble means "not proud" and "near the ground." This describes Wilbur perfectly. (NOTE: These meanings for "humble" are derived from two Latin words: *humilis*, meaning "low or lowly"; and *humus*, meaning "ground.")

3. What three things does Charlotte do at the fair that are unusual?

   She refuses to sing Wilbur a song, she leaves her web, and she states that she is making something for herself.

4. Refer to the second quotation. What sights and sounds does Charlotte say will show that morning has come?

   Charlotte says morning has come when light comes into the sky, sparrows sing, cows rattle their chains, the rooster crows, stars fade, and cars begin moving on the highway.

## Quotations

*The grownups climbed slowly into the truck and Wilbur heard the engine start and then heard the truck moving away in low speed. He would have felt lonely and homesick, had Charlotte not been with him. He never felt lonely when she was near.*

*"I'll tell you in the morning," she said. "When the first light comes into the sky and the sparrows stir and the cows rattle their chains, when the rooster crows and the stars fade, when early cars whisper along the highway, you look up here and I'll show you something. I will show you my masterpiece."*

## Discussion Questions

1. Find Dr. Dorian's prediction about Fern in Chapter 14. In what way does it come true in this chapter?
2. Consider the old sheep's prediction of the fair in Chapter 16. Compare the prediction to Templeton's experience in this chapter. Look for specific examples.

## Enrichment

**Character Pyramids - Wilbur and Charlotte:** Fill in the pyramids below using one descriptive word in each blank to answer the corresponding statements.

| Wilbur | Charlotte |
|---|---|
| panic | plan |

one word telling how they react to the news of Wilbur's death

| Wilbur | Charlotte |
|---|---|
| caring, providers | gullible, a threat |

two words relating their attitude about humans

| Wilbur | Charlotte |
|---|---|
| needy, self-centered, concerned | reliable, self-sacrificing, motherly |

three words revealing the kind of friend they are

| Wilbur | Charlotte |
|---|---|
| dependent, fearful, dramatic, humble | independent, wise, calm, confident |

four words describing their personality

## Reading Notes

| | |
|---|---|
| **nifty** | slang expression for "excellent" or "fine" |
| **magnum opus** | Latin phrase meaning "great work" |
| **acute attack of indigestion** | severe case of abdominal pain due to overeating |

## Vocabulary

1. I don't feel good at all. I think I'm **languishing**. growing weak
2. people would pass by … **marveling** at the miracle. looking in awe
3. he said in a **husky** voice. hoarse
4. What feasting and **carousing**! rowdy celebration
5. A real **gorge**! I must have eaten the remains of thirty lunches. a binge of overeating

## Comprehension Questions

1. Describe Charlotte's egg sac. Why does she call it her *magnum opus*?

   The egg sac looks something like a cocoon. It is peach-colored and looks like it is made of cotton candy. It is her masterpiece, the greatest thing she has ever made.

2. Describe the decline in Charlotte's behavior.

   She becomes weary, lacks energy, is focused only on her egg sac, and is awaiting her death.

3. What bad news does Templeton share after his night of carousing?

   The pig named Uncle has won the first-prize ribbon.

4. What is Wilbur's response to Templeton's pronouncement of his coming death in this chapter? How is his reaction different than in previous chapters?

   Wilbur remains fairly calm and changes the subject. Earlier in the book Wilbur would have panicked.

5. Why are the Zuckermans and Arables so joyful despite Avery's news?

   The announcer has summoned them for a special award.

## Quotations

*Charlotte's web never looked more beautiful than it looked this morning. Each strand held dozens of bright drops of early morning dew. The light from the east struck it and made it all plain and clear. it was a perfect piece of designing and building.*

*Up overhead, in the shadows of the ceiling, Charlotte crouched unseen, her front legs encircling her egg sac. Her heart was not beating as strongly as usual and she felt weary and old, but she was sure at last that she had saved Wilbur's life, and she felt peaceful and contented.*

## Discussion Questions

1. Where in *Charlotte's Web* have you seen similar imagery as in the first paragraph of this chapter? Why do you think the author chose to repeat this imagery?
2. *At the beginning of the book, Wilbur was worried about his future and focused on his own problems. How does this chapter show that Wilbur has learned to be a better friend to Charlotte? What elements of friendship does Charlotte continue to display?

## Enrichment

**Focus Passage - Dialogue:** Recall that **dialogue** is used to show a character's exact words. Each time a different character begins to speak, a new paragraph is begun and indented.

Directions: Copy the paragraphs of dialogue on page 144 (beginning with "Are you awake ..." through "... *magnum opus*."). Spelling, punctuation, and capitalization should be perfect.

## Reading Notes

| | |
|---|---|
| **hour of triumph** | a time of great victory |
| **ladeez** | exaggerated pronunciation for "ladies" |
| **phenomenon** | an extraordinary event |

## Vocabulary

1. said the loud speaker in a **pompous** voice. full of exaggerated pride
2. we now present Mr. Homer L. Zuckerman's **distinguished** pig. special
3. calling the attention of all and **sundry** to the fact various
4. In the last **analysis**, we simply know examination; study
5. The pain **revived** Wilbur. restored to consciousness

## Comprehension Questions

1. What does Fern prefer to do rather than watch the award ceremony?

   Fern prefers to ride the Ferris wheel with Henry Fussy.

2. Why does Wilbur receive special recognition?

   Wilbur receives special recognition because of his fame due to Charlotte's message about him.

3. How does Wilbur react to the attention?

   Wilbur faints, but he enjoys all the attention.

4. What does Avery do to get the crowd's attention? How do you know Avery enjoys being in the spotlight?

   Avery pretends to be a clown taking a shower. We know he enjoys being the center of attention because all he hears is the applause of the crowd. (see second to last paragraph of chapter)

## Quotations

*"Note the general radiance of this animal! Then remember the day when the word 'radiant' appeared clearly on the web. Whence came this mysterious writing? Not from the spider, we can rest assured of that. Spiders are very clever at weaving their webs, but needless to say spiders cannot write."*

Who said this? the "loudspeaker" On what occasion? awarding the special prize

*A great feeling of happiness swept over the Zuckermans and the Arables. This was the greatest moment in Mr. Zuckerman's life. It is deeply satisfying to win a prize in front of a lot of people.*

## Discussion Questions

1. *This chapter is titled "The Hour of Triumph." To whose triumph is the author referring?
2. What was Templeton's reason for biting Wilbur's tail?
3. Describe the scene after the photographer takes pictures of the event.

## Enrichment

**Dictation:** Listen carefully as your teacher reads the paragraphs of dialogue on page 156 (beginning with "Can't you see I'm busy ..." through "... don't point."). During the reading, write down what you hear. Then go back and make any necessary corrections in spelling, punctuation, or capitalization. When you are finished, compare your paragraph to the book and circle any errors.

REMEMBER! Indent and begin a new paragraph each time a different character begins to speak.

Note for instructor: Students should have their books closed during dictation. The passage should be read aloud only two times.

The first time the students write as much as they can, skipping a space if they miss a word. The second time students should fill in any blank spaces they may have and check for accuracy. Allow some time for them to make corrections in spelling, etc. They then should check their own work, using the passage in the book, circling or correcting any errors.

DICTATE:

"Can't you see I'm busy?" replied Avery in disgust.

"Look!" cried Fern, pointing. "There's Henry!"

"Don't shout, Fern!" said her mother. "And don't point!"

## Reading Notes

**monkeyshine** a playful trick
**wisecrack** a short, witty joke poking fun at someone

## Vocabulary

1. Your future is **assured**. guaranteed; certain
2. I thought you were cruel and **bloodthirsty**! violent
3. I was trying to lift up my life a **trifle**. small degree
4. And I thank you for your generous **sentiments**. statements based on emotions
5. Great sobs **racked** his body. shook
6. He heaved and grunted with **desolation**. loneliness

## Comprehension Questions

1. How has Wilbur lifted up Charlotte's life a trifle?

   He has been her friend. By helping to save Wilbur, Charlotte's life has become more meaningful than it would have been without Wilbur.

2. What has Wilbur learned from Charlotte?

   Wilbur has learned to reserve judgment when meeting new friends and to be willing to make sacrifices for others.

3. What is Templeton's role in Wilbur's plan? How does Wilbur convince him to help?

   Templeton is the only one who can climb up and retrieve Charlotte's egg sac. Wilbur promises to let him eat first from the trough each day.

4. How does Wilbur transport the egg sac? Why is he so confident in this method?

   He transports the egg sac in his mouth, because he knows it is waterproof and protected there.

# Quotations

*"Your success in the ring this morning was, to a small degree,* ***my*** *success. Your future is assured. You will live, secure and safe, Wilbur. Nothing can harm you now."*

Who said this? Charlotte

*But as he was being shoved into the crate, he looked up at Charlotte and gave her a wink. She knew he was saying good-bye in the only way he could. And she knew her children were safe.*

# Discussion Questions

1. *How has Templeton contributed to saving Wilbur's life? What is his attitude about helping?
2. *Describe the last moments Charlotte and Wilbur spend together.
3. *Reread the last paragraph of the chapter. What sad event occurs? How does the description of the activities at the fair grounds affect the mood of the paragraph?

# Enrichment

**Quotation Review:** How good is your memory? Supply the name of the speaker for each quotation below. The quotations are taken from Chapters 16-21.

1. "A fair is a rat's paradise. Everybody spills food at a fair." old sheep
2. "I think I'm going to faint." Wilbur
3. "I am going to give that pig a buttermilk bath." Mrs. Zuckerman
4. "What did you think I was, a spring chicken?" Uncle
5. "I don't feel good at all. I think I'm languishing, to tell you the truth." Charlotte
6. "I must have eaten the remains of thirty lunches." Templeton
7. "Henry invited me to go on the Ferris wheel again …" Fern
8. "You asked for water." Lurvy
9. "Humble, now isn't that just the word for Wilbur." Mr. Zuckerman
10. "Look at this! This pig has won first prize already." Avery

## Reading Notes

| | |
|---|---|
| **lee** | the side of an object that is sheltered from the wind |
| **Aranea** | Latin word for "spider" |
| **garrulous** | given to excessive, rambling talk; tiresomely talkative |
| **in a class by herself** | a category of her own; no one could match her |

## Vocabulary

1. "The most fun there is," **retorted** Fern, "is when the Ferris wheel stops ..." replied
2. whenever he found a **trinket** or a keepsake he carried it home decorative object of low value
3. in **shrill** chorus, came the voices of ... little frogs. high-pitched noise
4. We're leaving here on the warm **updraft**. upward current of air
5. You have chosen a **hallowed** doorway honorable
6. And many more happy, **tranquil** days followed. calm; peaceful

## Comprehension Questions

1. Describe the barn upon Wilbur's return. The barn feels like home to Wilbur. It smells good, his "beloved manure pile" is there, and Mr. Zuckerman hangs his medal on a nail over his pen.
2. How does Wilbur prepare for the birth of Charlotte's children? He places the egg sac close to himself in the warm manure. He warms it with his breath on cold nights. Then, he waits patiently.
3. What is Wilbur's reaction when the baby spiders are born? He trembles with excitement, squeals, races around, does a flip, and tells them how happy he is to see them. He offers to get them anything they need.
4. Why is Wilbur so sad several days after Charlotte's children are born? The baby spiders make web balloons and float away to find new homes. All of the new friends he thought he would have are now leaving him.

## Quotations

*Mr. Zuckerman took fine care of Wilbur all the rest of his days, and the pig was often visited by friends and admirers, for nobody ever forgot the year of his triumph and the miracle of the web.*

*Wilbur never forgot Charlotte. Although he loved her children and grandchildren dearly, none of the new spiders ever quite took her place in his heart. She was in a class by herself. It is not often that someone comes along who is a true friend and a good writer. Charlotte was both.*

## Discussion Questions

1. What seasonal changes occur on the farm in the winter and in the early spring?
2. *How does Wilbur's treatment of the baby spiders reflect character qualities he learned from Charlotte?
3. *Describe the changes that have occurred in Wilbur since the beginning of the book.

## Enrichment

**Composition:** In your own words write a paragraph (3-5 sentences) describing your favorite character from *Charlotte's Web*. Include details about the character's appearance and personality, and explain *why* you like this character. When you are finished writing, correct any errors in spelling, punctuation, and capitalization.

# Elements of Literature

Write sentences about the story.

## Character

**Character** means who is in the story.

1. Write one sentence describing a change in Wilbur. ______________________

   Answers will vary.

2. Write one sentence describing a change in Charlotte. ______________________

   Answers will vary.

## Setting

**Setting** means the time and place in which the story happens.

1. Write two sentences describing the County Fair. ______________________

   Answers will vary.

   ______________________

   ______________________

   ______________________

## Plot

**Plot** means action or what happens in the story.

Directions: Sequence the events in order. Then, copy them in order onto the following page. Each event should be written below a separate box. Finally, illustrate each event in the box.

**Events:**

__2__ Charlotte meets Wilbur's competition.

__4__ Charlotte reveals her *magnum opus.*

__6__ Charlotte's babies are born.

__1__ Before leaving the farm, Wilbur gets a buttermilk bath.

__3__ Templeton supplies the final web word.

__5__ Wilbur faints while receiving his award.

# Storyboard

1

Before leaving the farm, Wilbur gets a buttermilk bath.

2

Charlotte meets Wilbur's competition.

3

Templeton supplies the final web word.

4

Charlotte reveals her magnum opus.

5

Wilbur faints while receiving his award.

6

Charlotte's babies are born.

# Vocabulary

Write the letter of the vocabulary word on the line in front of its definition.

| | | |
|---|---|---|
| 1. l | greatest work | a. shrill |
| 2. a | high-pitched noise | b. listless |
| 3. o | struggle | c. keen |
| 4. j | growing weak | d. husky |
| 5. k | exceed; go beyond | e. gorge |
| 6. h | tiredly | f. trifle |
| 7. p | loneliness | g. revive |
| 8. m | full of exaggerated pride | h. wearily |
| 9. n | replied | i. sentiments |
| 10. c | sharp; highly developed | j. languishing |
| 11. q | spoke in a scornful manner | k. surpass |
| 12. g | restore to consciousness | l. masterpiece |
| 13. i | statements based on emotions | m. pompous |
| 14. d | hoarse | n. retorted |
| 15. s | to move upward | o. tussle |
| 16. t | special | p. desolation |
| 17. e | a binge of overeating | q. sneered |
| 18. r | disappeared | r. vanished |
| 19. f | small degree | s. ascend |
| 20. b | tired; no energy | t. distinguished |

# Short Answer

Answer the following questions in complete sentences.

1. What is the last word Charlotte weaves into her web, and why is it a perfect choice?

   The last word is "humble." It is the perfect choice because it means "near the ground" and "not proud"; Wilbur is both.

2. Describe Charlotte's egg sac. Why does she call it her *magnum opus?*

   The egg sac looks like a cocoon; it is peach-colored and looks like cotton candy. It is her masterpiece, the greatest thing she has ever made.

3. How do Charlotte and Wilbur spend their last moments together?

   They acknowledge their friendship. Wilbur says that Charlotte saved his life and pledges his willingness to give his life for her. Wilbur winks at Charlotte with her egg sac safely in his mouth.

4. How does Wilbur prepare for the birth of Charlotte's children?

   He places the egg sac close to himself in the warm manure. He warms it with his breath on cold nights. Then, he waits patiently for them to hatch.

5. Describe two changes that have occurred in Wilbur since the beginning of the book.

   Possible answers: He has learned the true meaning of friendship, he has learned not to make judgments about others, he has learned to accept others as they are and to appreciate them, he has learned selflessness, contentment, and how to get along with difficult people.

# Vocabulary Crossword

Use your vocabulary knowledge from reading *Charlotte's Web* to complete the following crossword:

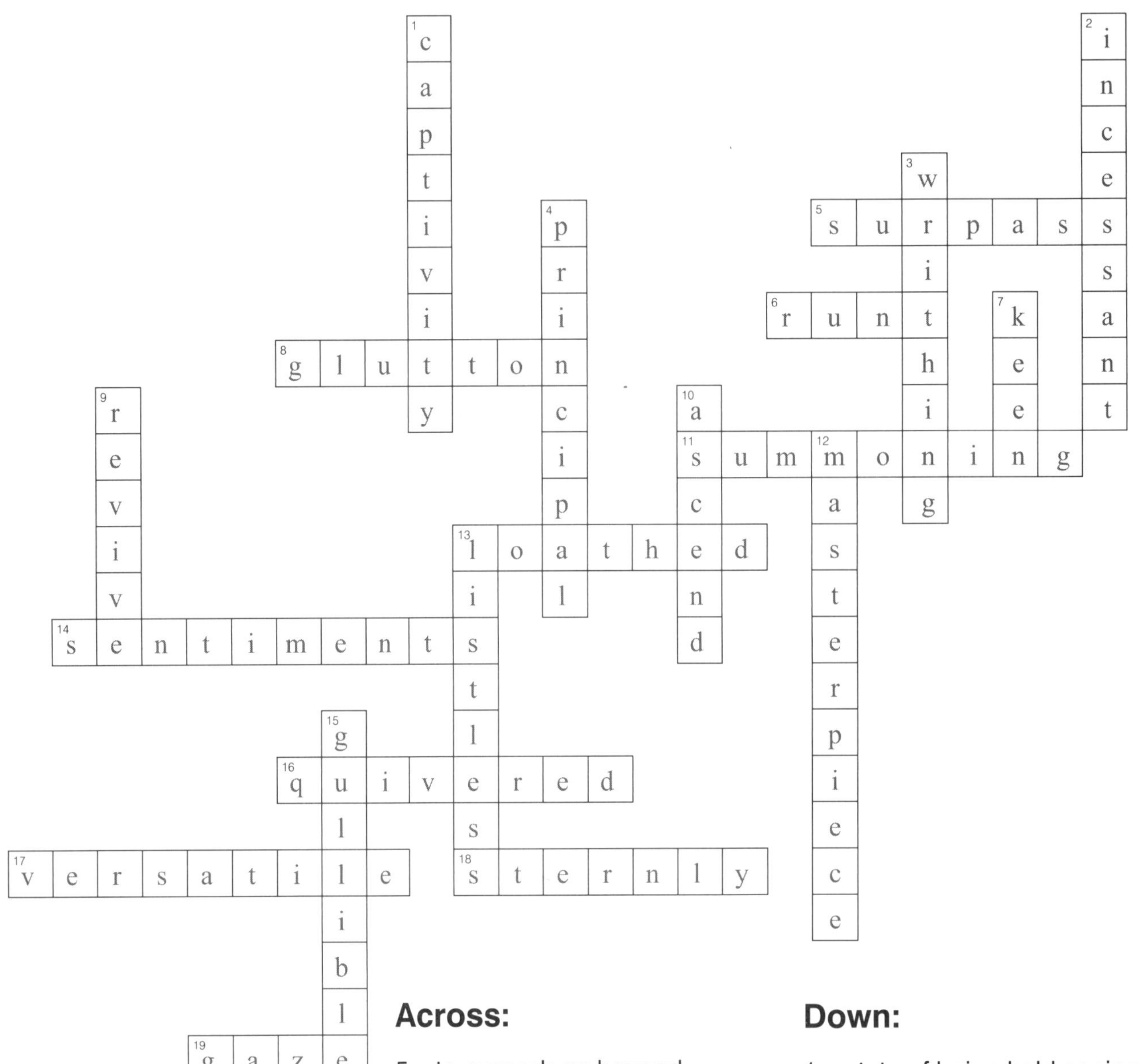


## Across:

5. to exceed; go beyond
6. smallest of the litter
8. one who habitually overeats
11. gathering, calling up
13. strongly disliked
14. statements based on emotions
16. trembled
17. adaptable; can adjust easily
18. seriously; firmly
19. to look at steadily

## Down:

1. state of being held against your will
2. endless; continuous
3. squirming
4. main; primary
7. sharp; highly developed
9. to restore to consciousness
10. to move upward
12. greatest work
13. tired; no energy
15. easily deceived

**Word Bank**

| | |
|---|---|
| runt | sternly |
| gaze | incessant |
| captivity | versatile |
| glutton | surpass |
| loathed | ascend |
| summoning | listless |
| gullible | keen |
| principal | masterpiece |
| quivered | revive |
| writhing | sentiments |

## Character Identification

Using the name bank, match each name to a description and write the name on the line.

| Mr. Arable | Mrs. Zuckerman | Fern | Lurvy | Charlotte |
|---|---|---|---|---|
| Wilbur | Templeton | goose | old sheep | Avery |

1. Wilbur ______ thought he was too young for freedom
2. old sheep ______ convinced Templeton that the fair is a rat's paradise
3. Templeton ______ a glutton, but not a merrymaker
4. Charlotte ______ believed people are gullible
5. Mr. Arable ______ only distributed pigs to early risers
6. Fern ______ was impressed with the stories of Charlotte's cousins
7. Lurvy ______ built a crate for Wilbur
8. Mrs. Zuckerman ______ believed that the spider was extraordinary, not the pig
9. goose ______ advised Wilbur during his escape
10. Avery ______ loved lots of attention and performed to get more of it

## Who Said That?

Write the name of the speaker on the line in front of each quotation.

1. goose ______ "No-no-no … It's the old pail trick, Wilbur. Don't fall for it!"
2. lamb ______ "Pigs mean less than nothing to me."
3. Mr. Zuckerman ______ "Humble, now isn't that just the word for Wilbur."
4. Avery ______ "Look at this! This pig has won first prize already."
5. Fern ______ "But it's unfair … The pig couldn't help being born small, could it?"
6. Wilbur ______ "I think I'm going to faint."
7. Lurvy ______ "You asked for water."
8. Charlotte ______ "I don't feel good at all. I think I'm languishing, to tell you the truth."
9. old sheep ______ "they're fattening you up because they're going to kill you"
10. Templeton ______ "I must have eaten the remains of thirty lunches."

## Multiple Choice

Choose the **best** answer for each question.

1. How is Templeton convinced to get words from the dump?
   - (a.) The old sheep points out that saving Wilbur means he will always have his leftover food to eat.
   - b. Templeton is finally convinced that it won't take much extra time or effort since he makes regular trips to the dump anyway.
   - c. The goose offers him another "dud" egg in the future if he will help Wilbur now.

2. What bad news is spreading in the barnyard?
   - a. Fern can't visit Wilbur any more.
   - (b.) Wilbur is going to be killed at Christmastime.
   - c. Templeton has captured a baby goose.

3. Why does Charlotte say she cannot go to the fair with Wilbur?
   - (a.) Nature says it is time to lay her eggs and she cannot delay it, not even for Wilbur.
   - b. She wants Wilbur to gain confidence by going alone and succeeding without further help.
   - c. She is confident her plan is working well and Wilbur no longer needs her help.

4. On what attribute does Charlotte rely to help her solve problems?
   - a. She relies on her willingness to work hard.
   - b. She depends on her intelligence; her ability to think of good ideas.
   - (c.) She depends on her ability to wait patiently.

5. How does Fern pamper Wilbur? **Both** must be true!
   - a. She gives him candy and lets him wade in the water.
   - b. She takes him for rides and lets him sleep in her bed.
   - (c.) She takes him for rides and lets him wade in the mud.

6. What advice does the old sheep give Wilbur before he is crated for the fair?
   - (a.) He tells Wilbur to struggle as the men try to put him into the crate.
   - b. He tells Wilbur to be sure to eat plenty of food before leaving because he may not get fed again until late in the evening.
   - c. He tells Wilbur to watch Charlotte carefully since she is so weak.

7. What does Charlotte do that Wilbur describes as "real thoughtful"?
   - (a.) She gives her prey an anaesthetic before drinking their blood.
   - b. She becomes his friend.
   - c. She captures flies so they won't bother other animals.

8. What is Wilbur's response to Templeton's pronouncement of Uncle's prize and Wilbur's death?
   (a.) Wilbur remains fairly calm and changes the subject.
   b. Wilbur starts to cry and asks Charlotte to tell him what to do.
   c. Wilbur panics and yells that he does not want to die.

9. What changes does Charlotte begin to notice in herself while at the fair?
   (a.) She feels a lack of energy and is tired all the time.
   b. She becomes very hungry and anxious to make a new web.
   c. She suddenly feels tired and hungry all the time.

10. Why is Wilbur so sad several days after Charlotte's children are born?
   (a.) The baby spiders make web balloons and float away to find new homes.
   b. He is lonely and bored because Fern no longer comes to visit.
   c. He misses Charlotte and wants to share the excitement of their birth with her.

## **Paragraph:** 3-5 sentences

In your own words write a paragraph describing your favorite character from *Charlotte's Web*. Include details about the character's appearance and personality. Also explain why you like this character. ___

_______________________________________________

Answers will vary.

_______________________________________________

_______________________________________________

_______________________________________________

_______________________________________________

_______________________________________________

_______________________________________________

_______________________________________________

**Short Answer:** Write a phrase or sentence for each question.

1. What does the word "arable" mean? Why is it a good name for a farm family?
"Arable" means land suitable for farming. It is a good name because the Arables are farmers.

2. Choose one minor character from the book (Mrs. Zuckerman, Dr. Dorian, Lurvy) and describe this person's reaction to Charlotte's web. Mrs. Zuckerman suspects the spider is special, not the pig; Lurvy is awestruck and kneels down to say a prayer; Dr. Dorian thinks any spider web is a miracle since they do it from instinct, not needing to be taught.

3. List three ways in which life on the Zuckerman farm changes as a result of Wilbur's fame.
Possible answers: people come to see Wilbur and the web, farm work is neglected, the Zuckermans and Lurvy dress up, Wilbur is fed more food and given clean straw.

4. Name one specific action Templeton does to help Wilbur and describe how it displays his selfishness. Possible answers: He gets words from the dump so he has Wilbur's leftovers to eat, he goes to the fair for all the promised food, he bites Wilbur's tail so Wilbur lives and he will continue to be fed, he rescues the egg sac after Wilbur promises he can eat first from his trough.

5. Describe one specific character quality that Wilbur learns from Charlotte and later displays toward her children. Self-sacrifice: he offers to help them however he can. He thinks of their needs ahead of his own and makes them a priority. He offers his friendship to them before he knows them well.

6. What is the overall plot of *Charlotte's Web*? What is the one central problem in the book and how is it solved? Possible answer: When a young runt pig is born, Fern rescues it from death, raises it, and sells it to her uncle. It soon becomes clear that Wilbur is merely being raised in order to be killed later at Christmastime. Wilbur's new friend, Charlotte, a spider, promises to save his life. She does this by weaving words that describe Wilbur into her web, causing people to see him differently, value him more, and decide not to kill him.

# Appendix

# BIOGRAPHICAL SKETCH

**Elwyn Brooks White (**1899-1985), was born on July 11, in Mount Vernon, New York. His father was a piano manufacturer, and while the family was not wealthy, they lived comfortably. As a young man, he attended Cornell University, graduating in 1921.

After college, he was offered a teaching position in Minnesota which he turned down. He desired to become a writer and felt periodicals might suit him better. He became a reporter for the *Seattle Times*. This did not turn out to be a good fit for him and he left the position after about two years. He was then employed by an advertising agency as a production assistant and copywriter. During this time of his career he enjoyed the publication of his first poems.

In 1925 he published his first article in *The New Yorker* magazine, which eventually led to a position as contributing editor in 1927. He continued as editor there throughout the rest of his life. This was a major influential change in his career as *The New Yorker* from the time of its origin was one of the nation's most prestigious periodicals, featuring many writing celebrities of the time.

He married Katherine Sergeant, a fellow editor, in 1929. They eventually had one son. In the years that followed, he published various poems, essays, and essay collections, as well as continuing his periodical contributions to *The New Yorker* and *Harper's* magazine.

White entered the field of children's literature in 1945 with the publication of *Stuart Little*. Years later, in 1952, he again turned to children's literature with the publication of *Charlotte's Web,* his most well-known work in this genre. This is the story of the unique friendship between a runt pig and a common barn spider. It sets forth for children enduring examples of loyalty and self-sacrifice in friendship, as well as serving as a gentle lesson on the reality of death.

E. B. White is also known for his association with William S. Strunk, Jr., a professor at Cornell during the years White was a student there. He took a course from Strunk, using a small book Strunk had written for the purpose. White later edited, revised, and contributed a chapter to this book, *The Elements of Style,* which was well received and became a widely used college text in subsequent years.

Around this time he began to receive multiple honors for his writing. These include the Laura Ingalls Wilder Medal for his children's books in 1970 and the National Medal for Literature in 1971. He was also elected to the American Academy of Arts and Letters in 1973. Still more publishing successes followed, including the children's book, *The Trumpet of the Swan,* in 1970 and various collections of his letters, essays, poems, and sketches.

E. B. White has been a great influence in the field of literature. His essays have served as models for generations of writers, and *the New Yorker*, considered by critics of his time to be a model of elegant, simple non-fiction, owes no small debt to White for its quality reputation.

# SPIDERS

Spiders are a member of the arachnid family, along with scorpions, mites, and ticks. They vary greatly in appearance; some are dull shades of gray or brown, others may be brilliant colors of red, yellow, or orange. Most spiders have a life span of two to three years.

All arachnid bodies consist of two parts—the head and the abdomen. They never have antennae or wings, but they do have eight jointed legs which are covered with hair that is sensitive to movement and used to help them grip the web. All spiders have fangs which produce venom for killing prey, and six to twelve eyes, though most have poor vision and rely on their ability to sense movement with their body hairs. A spider also has three or four pairs of spinnerets which produce silk. Liquid silk from inside the spider's body is sent out through these spinnerets to form many fine thin strands of thread which harden as they are exposed to the air and pulled on by the spider. Several strands joined together make up the sticky, durable lines of silk used to spin its web.

Not all spiders weave webs, but for those that do, the web serves as its means to capture prey for food. After the sticky web fibers have either attracted or captured its victim, the spider quickly approaches and wraps the prey with silk, immobilizing it. Since a spider cannot eat solid food, it must break it down before it is actually eaten. When the spider's fangs enter its prey, they inject poison and digestive juices into it. As these juices dissolve the body tissues, the spider simply drinks the resulting fluids out of its victim, leaving it to look undamaged on the outside. It later discards the inedible remains from the web.

Most spiders lay their eggs in a silk sac. Some carry this sac with them, others attach it to a web and camouflage it until the "spiderlings" are born. Since spiders do not have wings to carry them long distances, they must rely on different techniques to allow them to leave their original nest and form new homes. Many species use their silk threads as a sail with which to launch themselves into the wind to be carried to a new location. Others use "ballooning" which also relies on the wind; the spiderling stands in an exposed area, perhaps on the end of a branch, and lets out a droplet of silk. This drop is expanded and pulled by the wind, carrying the spider aloft, sometimes hundreds of miles away.

There are many different kinds of spiders. Each type has unique characteristics, life cycle, diet and style of web or home. Though varied in nature, most spiders are not harmful to people. Rather, they serve the important purpose of controlling harmful or destructive insects. The beauty and diversity displayed throughout the species is a vibrant reminder of God's awe-inspiring creativity.

## TO A FRIEND

by Grace Stricker Dawson

You entered my life in a casual way,
  And saw at a glance what I needed;
There were others who passed me or met me each day,
  But never a one of them heeded.
Perhaps you were thinking of other folks more,
  Or chance simply seemed to decree it;
I know there were many such chances before,
  But the others—well, they didn't see it.

You said just the thing that I wished you would say,
  And you made me believe that you meant it;
I held up my head in the old gallant way,
  And resolved you should never repent it.
There are times when encouragement means such a lot,
  And a word is enough to convey it;
There were others who could have, as easy as not—
  But, just the same, they didn't say it.

There may have been someone who could have done more
  To help me along, though I doubt it;
What I needed was cheering, and always before
  They had let me plod onward without it.
You helped to refashion the dream of my heart,
  And made me turn eagerly to it;
There were others who might have (I question that part)—
  But, after all, they didn't do it!

## THE SPIDER AND THE FLY

by Mary Howitt

"Will you walk into my parlour?" said the Spider to the Fly,
"'Tis the prettiest little parlour that ever you did spy;
The way into my parlour is up a winding stair,
And I've a many curious things to show when you are there."
"Oh no, no," said the little Fly, "to ask me is in vain,
For who goes up your winding stair can ne'er come down again."

"I'm sure you must be weary, dear, with soaring up so high;
Will you rest upon my little bed?" said the Spider to the Fly.
"There are pretty curtains drawn around; the sheets are fine and thin,
And if you like to rest awhile, I'll snugly tuck you in!"
"Oh no, no," said the little Fly, "for I've often heard it said,
They never, never wake again, who sleep upon your bed!"

Said the cunning Spider to the Fly, "Dear friend what can I do,
To prove the warm affection I've always felt for you?
I have within my pantry, good store of all that's nice;
I'm sure you're very welcome—will you please to take a slice?"
"Oh no, no," said the little Fly, "kind sir, that cannot be,
I've heard what's in your pantry, and I do not wish to see!"

"Sweet creature!" said the Spider, "you're witty and you're wise,
How handsome are your gauzy wings, how brilliant are your eyes!
I've a little looking-glass upon my parlour shelf,
If you'll step in one moment, dear, you shall behold yourself."
"I thank you, gentle sir," she said, "for what you're pleased to say,
And bidding you good morning now, I'll call another day."

The Spider turned him round about, and went into his den,
For well he knew the silly Fly would soon come back again:
So he wove a subtle web, in a little corner sly,
And set his table ready, to dine upon the Fly.
Then he came out to his door again, and merrily did sing,
"Come hither, hither, pretty Fly, with the pearl and silver wing;
Your robes are green and purple—there's a crest upon your head;
Your eyes are like the diamond bright, but mine are dull as lead!"

Alas, alas! how very soon this silly little Fly,
Hearing his wily, flattering words, came slowly flitting by;
With buzzing wings she hung aloft, then near and nearer drew,
Thinking only of her brilliant eyes, and green and purple hue—
Thinking only of her crested head—poor foolish thing! At last,
Up jumped the cunning Spider, and fiercely held her fast.
He dragged her up his winding stair, into his dismal den,
Within his little parlour—but she ne'er came out again!

And now, dear little children, who may this story read,
To idle, silly, flattering words, I pray you ne'er give heed:
Unto an evil counselor, close heart and ear and eye,
And take a lesson from this tale, of the Spider and the Fly.

# THE SPIDER'S WEB

## (A Natural History)

by E. B. White

The spider, dropping down from twig,
Unfolds a plan of her devising,
A thin premeditated rig
To use in rising.

And all that journey down through space,
In cool descent and loyal hearted,
She spins a ladder to the place
From where she started.

Thus I, gone forth as spiders do
In spider's web a truth discerning,
Attach one silken thread to you
For my returning.

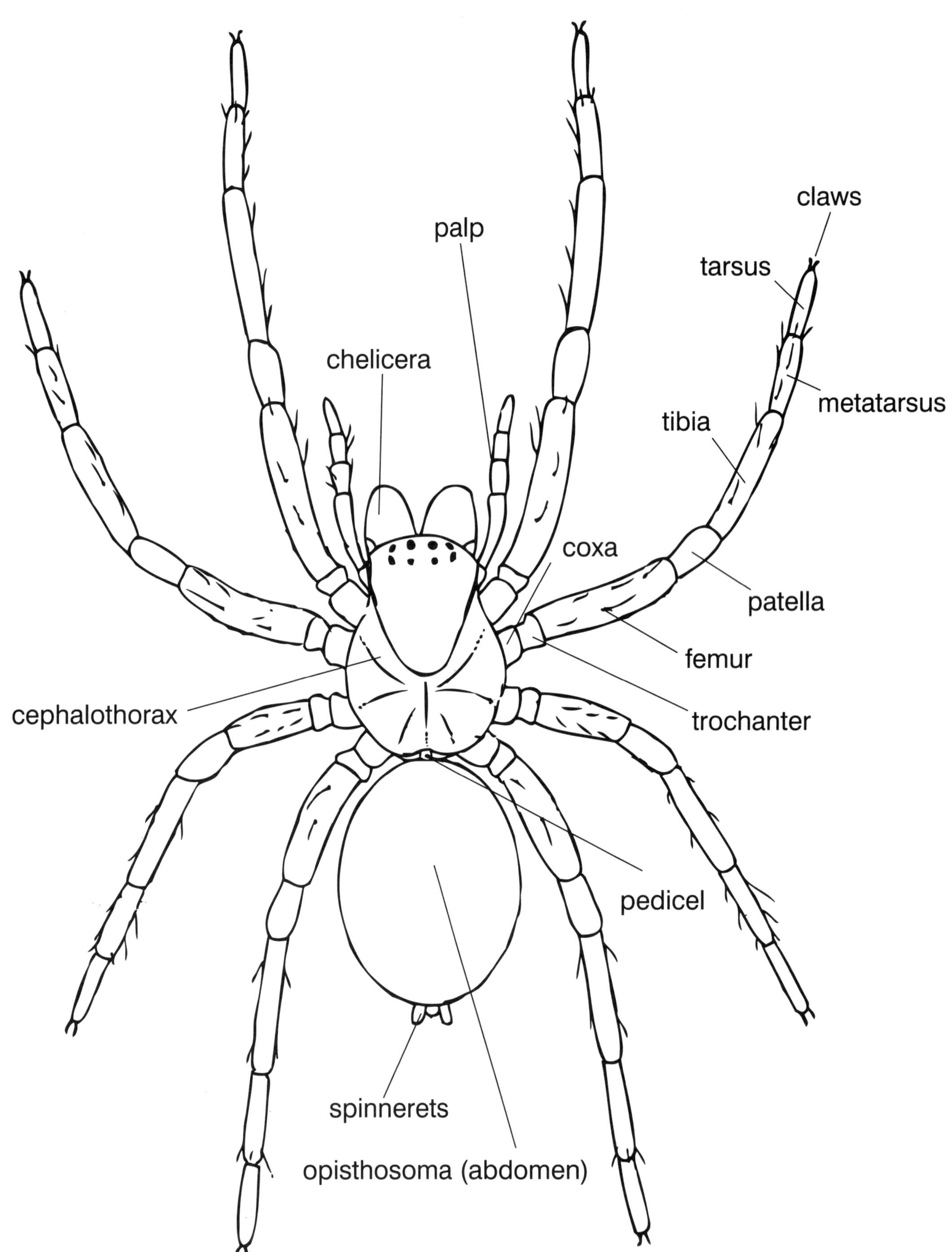
claws
palp
tarsus
chelicera
metatarsus
tibia
coxa
patella
femur
cephalothorax
trochanter
pedicel
spinnerets
opisthosoma (abdomen)

# Discussion Questions
# Answer Key

Discussion questions that have a * are NECESSARY to discuss with students as they may appear on a test and are generally important in understanding the full flavor of the story.

## Chapter I

1. What does the word "arable" mean? From what Latin word does "arable" come? Why is it a good name for a farm family?

   "Arable" means land suitable for farming. It is derived from the Latin arabilis meaning "to plow." It is a good name because the Arables are farmers.

2. Study the pictures on pages 5 and 6. How has the illustrator contrasted Avery and Fern?

   Answers will vary.

3. Reread Fern's objection to the runt's death and Mr. Arable's reply in the first quote above. In what way is a pig different than a little girl? Who do you agree with, and why?

   Human children have more intrinsic value than animals. Other answers will vary.

## Chapter II

1. Since straw is not a main source of food, what is it used for on a farm?

   On a farm, straw is often used for bedding and warmth.

2. Why is Fern's father able to predict what Wilbur will do to stay warm in his wooden box?

   Mr. Arable is an experienced farmer who knows the behavior and habits of his farm animals.

3. Why does Wilbur enjoy playing in the mud that is "delightfully sticky and oozy"?

   Wilbur is a pig. Pigs enjoy the coolness of the mud.

4. What reasons does Father give for insisting that Fern sell Wilbur?

   Wilbur is beginning to eat more food. Mr. Arable is not willing to provide food for him any longer because the cost of the food would be more than the price he could get selling him later. Mr. Arable has already sold Wilbur's siblings.

## Chapter III

1. Describe the barn; how it looks, what it contains, and how it feels.

   The barn is large and old. It smells of hay, manure, and animals. It even smells peaceful. It smells of the grain being stored in it, and other tools or items used for farming. It sometimes smells of fish. Mostly it smells of hay. It's warm in winter and cool in summer. There are many stalls and animals pens. You can find almost any kind of large or small tool you might need in the barn. Birds like to build nests in it and children like to play in it.

2. List the animals living in the barn. Describe the homes of each.

   The sheep and geese live in a sheepfold, and the pig lives in a pen below the main floor of the barn. The horses and cows live on the main floor of the barn, the horses in stalls, and the cows in tie-ups.

3. Explain the goose's warning: "He's appealing to your stomach."

   The goose is saying that Mr. Zuckerman is using food as a temptation in order to gain control over Wilbur.

4. What causes Wilbur to change his mind about being free? What does he long for?

   Wilbur changes his mind because he is being chased by everyone and he becomes confused. He longs for the safety and quiet of his pen. He wants Fern to hold him and comfort him.

**Chapter IV**

1. Which of the illustrations in Chapter 4 shows Wilbur at his saddest? How can you tell?

   Wilbur looks saddest in the second illustration, on page 31. He is laying flat on the ground, his mouth is open, and tears are visible. He is sobbing.

2. Who says, "Pigs mean less than nothing to me"? How does Wilbur respond to this statement?

   The lamb says this. Wilbur retorts that something that exists cannot be less than nothing.

3. In the second quote above, what does Templeton mean by "I am a glutton but not a merrymaker"?

   It means that even though he enjoys overeating, he does not enjoy frolicking or playing.

4. What does Lurvy do to try to make Wilbur feel better? Why?

   Lurvy gives Wilbur a mixture of sulphur and molasses as a means to help him regain his appetite.

**Chapter V**

1. Before Charlotte greets him, Wilbur is impatient, embarrassed, and humble. Describe how Wilbur demonstrates these qualities toward the beginning of the chapter.

   Wilbur shows impatience when he loudly addresses all the animals in the barn. He is embarrassed when everyone stares at him. He is humble when he quickly apologizes for awakening the other animals too early.

2. Describe in detail Charlotte's process for obtaining food.

   First, she dives at the insect. Next, she wraps it in silk. Then, she knocks it out by biting it. Finally, she eats it when she is ready for a meal.

3. Contrast how Charlotte obtains her food compared to how Wilbur receives his. What does this say about Charlotte?

   Charlotte has to work hard for her food, while Wilbur has his brought to him without any effort on his part. She is a hard and clever worker.

4. Explain Wilbur's statement, "… what a gamble friendship is!" in the first quote above.

   When you first befriend someone, you don't really know them well and the friendship may or may not work out. You need to be willing to get to know the other person instead of dismissing them because you have differences. You need to make an effort to find out what type of person your new friend is.

**Chapter VI**

1. List four birds mentioned in the chapter. Describe each bird's song.

   The book mentions the white-throated sparrow which says "peabody!", the phoebe which says "phoe-bee!", the song sparrow which says "sweet interlude," and the swallow which says "cheeky!"

2. Explain the statement, "A rotten egg is a regular stink bomb."

   A rotten egg, when broken, releases a strong, unbearable stench of sulphur.

### Chapter VII

3. Think about the first quote above and the first few paragraphs of the chapter. How has Wilbur's opinion of Charlotte's activities changed?

   Wilbur previously thought that Charlotte's activities were cruel and bloodthirsty. Now he views them as sensible and useful.

4. Reread the second quote above. How has Wilbur's outlook on life been altered since his earlier days on the farm?

   In his early days on the farm, Wilbur was bored and lonely. He didn't enjoy his life in the barn. Now he desperately wants to live so he can be in his home with his friends. (See Chapters 3 and 4 for comparison.)

### Chapter VIII

1. What is your opinion about talking animals?

   Answers will vary.

### Chapter IX

1. In this chapter, Wilbur tries several times to accomplish something that he was not made to do. How can we discover our own unique gifts and talents? How can we encourage our friends and family to do the same?

   We can try different activities to see if they are something we enjoy and whether or not we can succeed at them. Charlotte lets Wilbur try to spin the web even though she knows he can't do it. She enjoys seeing he is not a quitter. We can encourage our family and friends to try new things even when we think they won't be successful.

2. What observations does Charlotte make about people in this chapter? Do you think she is correct in her assumptions?

   Charlotte observes that men rush back and forth and do not spend much time quietly thinking. They are always looking for something better instead of being satisfied with what they have and waiting patiently for whatever comes. Answers will vary.

### Chapter X

1. Reread the second quote above. Has Wilbur done anything to earn or deserve Charlotte's affection? What does that say about the nature of friendship?

   No; we can choose to be a friend to someone who needs a friend whether or not we receive any benefit from their friendship. A good friend does not expect anything in return.

2. In what ways are Templeton, the goose, and Lurvy "accidental" heroes?

   Templeton wanted to save the rotten goose egg for his collection. The goose laid the egg and allowed Templeton to take it. Lurvy saved the barn from the smell by burying the broken egg.

3. Describe the highlights of Fern's and Avery's day at the Zuckerman farm.

   The children ate pie, played on the swing, played with a frog, and picked and ate raspberries.

## Chapter XI

1. In the previous chapter, Charlotte said that humans are gullible. Give examples of specific ways from this chapter that prove Charlotte was correct in her observation.

   Mr. Zuckerman and Lurvy both notice that Wilbur is "solid" and "extra good". The minister encourages the congregation to always be on the watch for the coming of wonders. Suddenly, people come from miles around to admire Wilbur.

2. Why do the Zuckermans and Lurvy change their personal appearance and habits once Wilbur becomes famous?

   They know they are being watched so they want to make a good impression. Wilbur's fame brings attention to the farm which increases the family's care and respect for him.

## Chapter XII

1. Reread the first quote above. Why is Charlotte so confident that her plan to save Wilbur will work?

   She is confident because of the way in which people have reacted to the first web. Their reactions show that they believe Wilbur is special.

2. What is Wilbur's reaction to the new word? What does this show about his character?

   Wilbur blushes and says he is just an average pig. This reaction shows that he is humble.

3. Why are some words italicized in the last two paragraphs of the chapter?

   The words are italicized for emphasis.

## Chapter XIII

1. List some of the things Templeton finds in the dump.

   Templeton finds bottles, tin cans, rags, hinges, springs, dead batteries, mops, clothes, and pails.

2. Describe some of the amazing qualities and abilities of Charlotte's relatives.

   Charlotte's relatives have caught a fish in a web and have made a web balloon with which to fly.

## Chapter XIV

1. Refer to the second quote above. How does Dr. Dorian explain the difference between the "miracle" of a spider web and the fact that Mrs. Arable can crochet a doily and knit a sock?

   Someone taught Mrs. Arable how to crochet and knit, but nobody taught a spider how to weave a web. Spiders are born knowing how to make webs.

2. Contrast Mrs. Arable's and Dr. Dorian's attitudes about things they do not understand. Is there something you don't like because you don't understand it? How could you change your opinion?

   Dr. Dorian admits he does not understand everything, but has decided not to let it bother him. However, Mrs. Arable does not like things that she cannot understand. Answers will vary.

### Chapter XV

1. A Lesson in Friendship: Reread the second quote above. Describe how the following characters showed true friendship to Wilbur: Charlotte, Fern, the goose, the old sheep.

   Charlotte gave her friendship and help freely, before she even knew Wilbur very well. (Ch. 4,5) She stood up for Wilbur when the lamb spoke harshly to him. (Ch. 9) She sacrifices her time and energy to help Wilbur each time she builds a new web. Fern saved Wilbur's life and took care of him. When he moved to Zuckerman's, she visited him regularly. The goose is consistently friendly and kind to Wilbur and tries to help by suggesting words for the web. The old sheep told Wilbur the truth about what was going to happen to him. (Ch. 7) She knew how to help Wilbur by convincing Templeton to help. (Ch. 12)

2. Describe some of the changes the farm experiences as the transition from summer to autumn begins.

   The crickets sing a summer's end song, school will soon begin, apples fall from the trees, it begins to frost, and it is potato digging time.

3. How does the book hint at some future event concerning Charlotte? Does it sound exciting or unpleasant?

   The book hints at the future because Charlotte is described as knowing that she doesn't have much time left and she has worries of her own. It causes us to ask ourselves, "What kind of other worries?" It feels at this point like this event may be unpleasant.

### Chapter XVI

1. Describe the dreams of Fern, Avery, Mr. and Mrs. Zuckerman, and Lurvy the night before the fair.

   Fern dreams of becoming sick in the swings; Avery dreams of riding the Ferris wheel; Lurvy dreams of winning an Indian blanket; Mrs. Zuckerman dreams of a deep freeze; Mr. Zuckerman dreams of a huge, prize-winning Wilbur.

2. Reread the first quote above. How do the words in the web continue to influence people's thinking about Wilbur?

   Each character uses a web word to describe Wilbur. The words from the web have helped to form their opinions of Wilbur.

3. Authors often use repetition to emphasize a point in a story. In what way does the author use repetition in this chapter to make the story more interesting?

   The author repeats the phrase "the geese cheered" seven times on pages 125-129. This supports the general characterization of geese as well as being amusing.

### Chapter XVII

1. Reread the second quote above, focusing on the last sentence. Why do you think Charlotte doesn't want to be noticed? What does she prefer?

   Charlotte doesn't like being in the spotlight and knows that being noticed can be dangerous to her. (i.e., Chapter 10, Avery tries to capture her.) She prefers drawing attention to Wilbur.

2. *What signs are there of Wilbur becoming a better friend towards Charlotte?

   Wilbur asks how Charlotte feels, sympathizes with her, makes suggestions for her well-being, and worries about her. He also lets her rest and does not ask her for anything.

3. Think back to the dreams in the beginning of Chapter 16. Did any of them come true in this chapter? Predict the outcome of Mr. Zuckerman's dream.

   Fern and Avery dreamed of playing on the midway rides and in this chapter they are able to play on the midway by themselves. Lurvy dreamed of winning a Navajo blanket, and in this chapter he does win one. Mrs. Zuckerman dreamed about a deep freeze unit, and in this chapter she looks at them. Mr. Zuckerman's dream has not yet come true, but the prizes will be awarded later, so it may still happen. Predictions will vary.

**Chapter XVIII**

1. Find Dr. Dorian's prediction about Fern in Chapter 14. In what way does it come true in this chapter?

   He predicted that Henry Fussy would catch Fern's attention. Henry Fussy and Fern enjoy riding the Ferris wheel together.

2. Consider the old sheep's prediction of the fair in Chapter 16. Compare the prediction to Templeton's experience in this chapter. Look for specific examples.

   The old sheep said there would be old discarded sandwiches, hard-boiled eggs, particles of cheese, and loot everywhere. It would be a rat's paradise. Templeton finds leftovers from someone's lunch, including a sandwich, a piece of Swiss cheese, part of a hard-boiled egg, and the core of a wormy apple. Templeton declares it is a "rat's paradise."

**Chapter XIX**

1. Where in *Charlotte's Web* have you seen similar imagery as in the first paragraph of this chapter? Why do you think the author chose to repeat this imagery?

   This imagery is seen at the end of Chapter 18. The author may have chosen to repeat this imagery to show continuity between chapters, to draw attention to beautiful language, or to show Charlotte's wisdom and knowledge.

2. At the beginning of the book, Wilbur was worried about his future and focused on his own problems. How does this chapter show that Wilbur has learned to be a better friend to Charlotte? What elements of friendship does Charlotte continue to display?

   Wilbur shares her joy in the accomplishment of her egg sac. He compliments her web and encourages her when she is downhearted. Charlotte distracts Wilbur from worrying and redirects his attention onto his coming triumph. She is happy despite her own approaching death because his safety is secure.

**Chapter XX**

1. This chapter is titled "The Hour of Triumph." To whose triumph is the author referring?

   This title could have a multiple meaning. It could refer to the triumph of the Zuckermans in winning the special award. It could also refer to Wilbur's triumph in winning the award. However, the primary meaning is one we know only as readers, Charlotte's triumph in knowing her plan succeeded and she has saved Wilbur's life.

2. What was Templeton's reason for biting Wilbur's tail?

   Templeton wanted to revive Wilbur so that he could receive the prize. The "loudspeaker" said they could not award a dead pig. If Wilbur didn't receive the prize, he may still be killed at Christmas and Templeton would no longer get his share of Wilbur's food.

3. Describe the scene after the photographer takes pictures of the event.

   Lurvy throws water on Mr. Zuckeman and Avery, and Avery clowns around for the crowd.

## Chapter XXI

1. How has Templeton contributed to saving Wilbur's life? What is his attitude about helping?

   Templeton got magazine clippings from the dump, saved Charlotte from Avery, and bites Wilbur's tail to revive him. He wants to be thanked and recognized for his work. He is the only character who complains about getting no credit for his work.

2. Describe the last moments Charlotte and Wilbur spend together.

   They acknowledge their friendship. Wilbur acknowledges that Charlotte saved his life and pledges his willingness to give his life for her. In their final parting, Wilbur winks at Charlotte with her egg sac safely in his mouth.

3. Reread the last paragraph of the chapter. What sad event occurs? How does the description of the activities at the fair grounds affect the mood of the paragraph?

   Charlotte dies alone. The details given in the paragraph explain the loneliness and emptiness of the fair. (Everyone was leaving. The fair grounds were being dismantled and put away. The buildings were empty and forlorn. Trash was everywhere.) Therefore, the fair was coming to an end at the same time that Charlotte's life was ending.

## Chapter XXII

1. What seasonal changes occur on the farm in the winter and in the early spring?

   In winter (see p. 174), the temperature drops, snow falls, barn animals stay in or near the barn, Templeton moves inside, and the nights are cold. In the spring (see p. 176), the frogs begin croaking, lambs are born, the snow melts, streams and ditches bubble and chatter, birds arrive and sing, mornings come sooner, light strengthens, and the goose lays her eggs.

2. How does Wilbur's treatment of the baby spiders reflect character qualities he learned from Charlotte?

   He asks them if he can get them anything. He is thinking of their needs ahead of his own and making them a priority. He offers his friendship to them before he really even knows them. Charlotte did these same things for him when they first met.

3. Describe the changes that have occurred in Wilbur since the beginning of the book.

   1. Wilbur has grown and matured, due in part to Charlotte's influence. 2. He has learned the true meaning of friendship. 3. He has learned not to make judgments about others. 4. He has learned to accept others as they are and to appreciate them. 5. He has learned selflessness and the need for dependence on others in life. 6. He has learned to love. 7. He has learned to be content. 8. He has learned how to get along with difficult people (ie., Templeton).

# Quizzes & Final Test

(reproducible for classroom use)

# Charlotte's Web Quiz 1
Chapters 1-7

Name ______________________

Date ______________________

Write the letter of the vocabulary word on the line in front of its definition.

| | | | |
|---|---|---|---|
| 1. ______ | state of being held against your will | a. | runt |
| 2. ______ | constant; neverending | b. | injustice |
| 3. ______ | unfairness | c. | gaze |
| 4. ______ | one who habitually overeats | d. | captivity |
| 5. ______ | strongly disliked | e. | commotion |
| 6. ______ | to bear, tolerate | f. | glutton |
| 7. ______ | smallest of the litter | g. | endure |
| 8. ______ | noisy, confused activity | h. | blundered |
| 9. ______ | moved carelessly | i. | unremitting |
| 10. ______ | to look at steadily | j. | loathed |

Match each name below with a character description.

| | | | | |
|---|---|---|---|---|
| **Mr. Arable** | **Mr. Zuckerman** | **goose** | **Wilbur** | **Charlotte** |
| **Lurvy** | **Templeton** | **Fern** | **old sheep** | **lamb** |

1. ______________________ only distributed pigs to early risers
2. ______________________ thought he was too young for freedom
3. ______________________ a glutton, but not a merrymaker
4. lam ______________________ believed that pigs were less than nothing
5. ______________________ first noticed something was wrong with the pig
6. ______________________ thoughtfully gave her victims an anaesthetic
7. ______________________ was treated as an equal by the animals in the barn
8. ______________________ bought Wilbur for $6.00
9. ______________________ spread the bad news about the conspiracy on the farm
10. ______________________ advised Wilbur during his escape

Choose the **best** answer for each question.

1. What is the first thing Fern teaches Wilbur?
   a. to take milk from a bottle
   b. to sleep in a baby carriage
   c. to follow her around the farm

2. How does Fern pamper Wilbur? **Both** must be true!
   a. She takes him for rides and lets him sleep in her bed.
   b. She takes him for rides and lets him wade in the mud.
   c. She gives him candy and lets him wade in the water.

3. Who is the first animal Wilbur meets?
   a. Templeton
   b. Charlotte
   c. the goose

4. Why does Wilbur so willingly follow the advice of the goose at first?
   a. He is curious and adventurous.
   b. He wants to visit Fern.
   c. He is bored and discouraged.

5. What is Wilbur's pleasant surprise at the end of the rainy day?
   a. Fern visits unexpectedly.
   b. He hears a voice offering him friendship.
   c. Lurvy brings him extra slops.

6. How does the author describe Charlotte?
   a. She is a large, gray spider, about the size of a gumdrop.
   b. She is a large, black spider, about the size of a penny.
   c. She is a large, brown spider, about the size of a grape.

7. What word does Charlotte use to greet Wilbur for the first time?
   a. "Hello!"
   b. "Greetings!"
   c. "Salutations!"

8. Where does Templeton put the "dud" goose egg?
    a. He rolls it to the dump.
    b. He rolls it to his lair under the trough.
    c. He rolls it to his lair under the farmhouse.

9. What does Charlotte do that Wilbur describes as "real thoughtful"?
    a. She gives her prey an anaesthetic before drinking their blood.
    b. She captures flies so they won't bother other animals.
    c. She becomes his friend.

10. What bad news is spreading in the barnyard?
    a. Templeton has captured a baby goose.
    b. Wilbur is going to be killed at Christmastime.
    c. Fern can't visit Wilbur anymore.

Answer the following questions in complete sentences.

---

1. What does the word "arable" mean? Why is it a good name for a farm family? ________________

_______________________________________________

_______________________________________________

2. What reasons did Father give for insisting that Fern sell Wilbur? ________________

_______________________________________________

_______________________________________________

_______________________________________________

_______________________________________________

3. What important event, announced by Charlotte, happened in the barn cellar? ________________

_______________________________________________

4. Explain Wilbur's statement "… what a gamble friendship is!" ________________

_______________________________________________

_______________________________________________

_______________________________________________

_______________________________________________

5. What promise does Charlotte make to Wilbur? ________________

_______________________________________________

# Charlotte's Web Quiz 2

## Chapters 8-15

Name ______________________________

Date ______________________________

Write the letter of the vocabulary word on the line in front of its definition.

| | | |
|---|---|---|
| 1. ______ pleased; satisfied | a. | principal |
| 2. ______ gathering; calling up | b. | writhing |
| 3. ______ easily deceived | c. | summoning |
| 4. ______ unfriendly; bad-tempered | d. | versatile |
| 5. ______ main; primary | e. | surly |
| 6. ______ trembled | f. | sternly |
| 7. ______ squirming | g. | gratified |
| 8. ______ seriously; firmly | h. | quivered |
| 9. ______ endless; continuous | i. | gullible |
| 10. ______ adaptable; can adjust easily | j. | incessant |

Match each name below with a character description.

| | | | | |
|---|---|---|---|---|
| **Avery** | **Templeton** | **Fern** | **Mrs. Arable** | **Charlotte** |
| **Dr. Dorian** | **Mrs. Zuckerman** | **Wilbur** | **old sheep** | **Lurvy** |

1. ______________________________ believed that the spider was extraordinary, not the pig
2. ______________________________ built a crate for Wilbur
3. ______________________________ found the words "With New Radiant Action" at the dump
4. ______________________________ was impressed with the stories of Charlotte's cousins
5. ______________________________ worked hard to make a web, but failed
6. ______________________________ worried about Fern's claim to understand animals
7. ______________________________ tried to capture Charlotte, but failed
8. ______________________________ convinced Templeton to get new words from the dump
9. ______________________________ believed that people are very gullible
10. ______________________________ thought if people talked less, animals might talk more

Choose the **best** answer for each question.

1. How does Wilbur try to imitate Charlotte?
   a. He offers friendship to a baby goose.
   b. He catches some flies and eats them.
   c. He tries to spin a web of his own.

2. Why does Charlotte think her webs are better than human "webs"?
   a. Her webs are more easily changed and therefore more creative.
   b. Her webs are built faster and are more practical.
   c. Her webs are more beautiful to look at.

3. On what attribute does Charlotte rely to help her solve problems?
   a. She depends on her ability to wait patiently.
   b. She relies on her willingness to work hard.
   c. She depends on her intelligence; her ability to think of good ideas.

4. What catastrophe is prevented from happening in the barn cellar?
   a. Charlotte gets caught by Avery.
   b. The baby geese get loose in the barnyard.
   c. Fern is no longer allowed to visit Wilbur.

5. Who is the first person to discover the "miracle" web?
   a. Mr. Zuckerman
   b. Lurvy
   c. Fern

6. How is Mrs. Zuckerman's view of the "miracle" web different from everyone else's view of it?
   a. She thinks the spider is special, not necessarily the pig.
   b. She is busy and doesn't take much interest in the web at all.
   c. She becomes very excited and plans to buy a deep freeze when they are famous.

7. How is Templeton convinced to get words from the dump?
   a. The goose offers him another "dud" egg in the future if he will help Wilbur now.
   b. Templeton is finally convinced that it won't take much extra time or effort since he makes regular trips to the dump anyway.
   c. The old sheep points out that saving Wilbur means he will always have his leftover food to eat.

8. How does Charlotte entertain herself while weaving?
    a. She talks to herself and cheers herself on as she weaves.
    b. She tells the other animals stories about her amazing cousins.
    c. She sings songs to Wilbur.

9. What does Dr. Dorian think about Fern's love of animals and spending so much time in the barn?
    a. He thinks it is dangerous, but he's not worried because she will soon grow out of it.
    b. He believes her love for animals is healthy and therefore is not worried about her.
    c. He agrees with Mrs. Arable that Fern should not be allowed to spend much time in the barn.

10. Why does Charlotte say she cannot go to the fair with Wilbur?
    a. Nature says it is time to lay her eggs and she cannot delay it, not even for Wilbur.
    b. She wants Wilbur to gain confidence by going alone and succeeding without further help.
    c. She is confident her plan is working well and Wilbur no longer needs her help.

Answer the following questions in complete sentences.

1. What plan does Charlotte come up with to save Wilbur's life? Why does she think it will work?____

_______________________________________________

_______________________________________________

2. Name two specific ways in which the webs affect life on the Zuckerman farm. ________________

_______________________________________________

_______________________________________________

_______________________________________________

3. What is Wilbur's reaction to the second word in the web ("terrific")? What does this show about his character? ________________________________

_______________________________________________

4. As summer comes to an end, what are Wilbur and Charlotte each looking forward to?__________

_______________________________________________

_______________________________________________

5. Choose one of the following characters and describe how they show friendship towards Wilbur. (Fern, the goose, the old sheep)______________________________

_______________________________________________

_______________________________________________

# Charlotte's Web Quiz 3
Chapters 16-22

Name ______________________________

Date ______________________________

Write the letter of the vocabulary word on the line in front of its definition.

| | | |
|---|---|---|
| 1. ______ to exceed; go beyond | | a. listless |
| 2. ______ to move upward | | b. gorge |
| 3. ______ tired, no energy | | c. sentiments |
| 4. ______ sharp; highly developed | | d. surpass |
| 5. ______ greatest work | | e. masterpiece |
| 6. ______ a binge of overeating | | f. desolation |
| 7. ______ to restore to consciousness | | g. ascend |
| 8. ______ statements based on emotions | | h. retorted |
| 9. ______ loneliness | | i. revive |
| 10. ______ replied | | j. keen |

Match each name below with a character description.

| | | | | |
|---|---|---|---|---|
| **Uncle** | **Mrs. Zuckerman** | **Avery** | **old sheep** | **Charlotte** |
| **Wilbur** | **Aranea** | **geese** | **Lurvy** | **Templeton** |

1. ______________________________ won a first prize blue ribbon at the fair
2. ______________________________ won an Indian blanket
3. ______________________________ convinced Templeton that the fair is a rat's paradise
4. ______________________________ fainted from all the attention
5. ______________________________ gorged himself at the fair
6. ______________________________ one of Charlotte's baby spiders
7. ______________________________ loved lots of attention and performed to get more of it
8. ______________________________ gave Wilbur a buttermilk bath
9. ______________________________ cheered
10. ______________________________ created her *magnum opus*

1. What special treatment does Wilbur get before departing for the fair?
   a. Wilbur receives extra slops in his trough.
   b. Wilbur gets a buttermilk bath.
   c. Wilbur is petted and very carefully lifted and placed into the crate.

2. What advice does the old sheep give Wilbur before he is crated for the fair?
   a. He tells Wilbur to struggle as the men try to put him into the crate.
   b. He tells Wilbur to be sure to eat plenty of food before leaving because he may not get fed again until late in the evening.
   c. He tells Wilbur to watch Charlotte carefully since she is so weak.

3. Why does Charlotte dislike Uncle?
   a. Charlotte sees how large he is and is concerned that he may win the prize.
   b. Charlotte dislikes Uncle because he tells weak jokes and has an unusual name.
   c. Charlotte thinks he is dirty, unpleasant in personality, and he tells weak jokes.

4. What changes does Charlotte begin to notice in herself while at the fair?
   a. She feels a lack of energy and is tired all the time.
   b. She becomes very hungry and anxious to make a new web.
   c. She suddenly feels tired and hungry all the time.

5. What does Charlotte do at the fair that is unusual? **Both** must be true!
   a. Charlotte leaves her web to hunt for flies in another corner of the barn.
   b. Charlotte refuses to sing Wilbur a song and she leaves her web.
   c. Charlotte tells Uncle stories about her cousins and makes something for herself.

6. What is Wilbur's response to Templeton's pronouncement of Uncle's prize and Wilbur's resulting death?
   a. Wilbur panics and yells that he does not want to die.
   b. Wilbur starts to cry and asks Charlotte to tell him what to do.
   c. Wilbur remains fairly calm and changes the subject.

7. What does Fern prefer to do rather than watch the award ceremony?
   a. Fern prefers to spend time and money in the midway.
   b. Fern prefers to sit quietly in the barn watching Charlotte.
   c. Fern prefers to ride the Ferris wheel with Henry Fussy.

8. How does Wilbur react to all the attention he receives when he gets his special award?
    a. He faints, but he enjoys all the attention.
    b. He hates all the attention because he is shy and modest.
    c. He loves all the attention and acts silly to make the people laugh.

9. How does Wilbur transport the egg sac?
    a. Wilbur rolls it carefully into his crate and buries it in the soft straw.
    b. Wilbur carries it in his mouth because he knows it is water proof.
    c. Wilbur makes a deal with Templeton to carry it since he doesn't have hands or paws.

10. Why is Wilbur so sad several days after Charlotte's children are born?
    a. He is lonely and bored because Fern no longer comes to visit.
    b. He misses Charlotte and wants to share the excitement of their birth with her.
    c. The baby spiders make web balloons and float away to find new homes.

Answer the following questions in complete sentences.

1. What is the last word Charlotte weaves into her web, and why is it a perfect choice? ____________

______________________________________________________________________

______________________________________________________________________

2. Describe Charlotte's egg sac. Why does she call it her *magnum opus*? ____________

______________________________________________________________________

______________________________________________________________________

______________________________________________________________________

3. How do Charlotte and Wilbur spend their last moments together? ____________

______________________________________________________________________

______________________________________________________________________

4. How does Wilbur prepare for the birth of Charlotte's children? ____________

______________________________________________________________________

______________________________________________________________________

5. Describe two changes that have occurred in Wilbur since the beginning of the book. ____________

______________________________________________________________________

______________________________________________________________________

______________________________________________________________________

# Charlotte's Web Final Test

Name ______________________

Date ______________________

**Vocabulary:** Write the letter of the vocabulary word next to its definition.

| | | |
|---|---|---|
| 1. ______ to look at steadily | a. listless |
| 2. ______ to restore to consciousness | b. summoning |
| 3. ______ easily deceived | c. quivered |
| 4. ______ endless; continuous | d. versatile |
| 5. ______ adaptable; can adjust easily | e. gaze |
| 6. ______ one who habitually overeats | f. incessant |
| 7. ______ trembled | g. revived |
| 8. ______ statements based on emotions | h. glutton |
| 9. ______ gathering; calling up | i. sentiments |
| 10. ______ tired; no energy | j. gullible |

**Character Identification:** Choose the name that matches each description and write it on the line.

| | | | | |
|---|---|---|---|---|
| **Fern** | **Templeton** | **Lurvy** | **Mrs. Arable** | **Wilbur** |
| **Dr. Dorian** | **Mrs. Zuckerman** | **goose** | **Charlotte** | **old sheep** |

1. ______________________ advised Wilbur during his escape
2. ______________________ a glutton, but not a merrymaker
3. ______________________ won an Indian blanket
4. ______________________ believed that people are very gullible
5. ______________________ was treated as an equal by the animals in the barn
6. ______________________ convinced Templeton to go to the dump and the fair
7. ______________________ worried about Fern's claim to understand animals
8. ______________________ thought if people talked less, animals might talk more
9. ______________________ worked hard to make a web, but failed
10. ______________________ believed that the spider was extraordinary, not the pig

## Who Said That?: Match each name to a quotation below and write the name on the line.

| Wilbur | Templeton | Fern | Charlotte | Uncle |
|---|---|---|---|---|
| lamb | Mr. Zuckerman | Mr. Arable | old sheep | goose |

1. ____________________ "Stop your crying! I can't stand hysterics."
2. ____________________ "I think I'm going to faint."
3. ____________________ "Humble, now isn't that just the word for Wilbur."
4. ____________________ "But it's unfair … The pig couldn't help being born small, could it?"
5. ____________________ "they're fattening you up because they're going to kill you"
6. ____________________ "Pigs mean less than nothing to me."
7. ____________________ "I only distribute pigs to early risers."
8. ____________________ "What did you think I was, a spring chicken?"
9. ____________________ "No-no-no … It's the old pail trick, Wilbur. Don't fall for it!"
10. ____________________ "I must have eaten the remains of thirty lunches."

## Dialogue: Add quotation marks in the following paragraphs where they are needed.

Salutations! it said. I'm up here.

So am I, said another tiny voice.

So am I, said a third voice. Three of us are staying. We like this place, and we like *you.*

Wilbur looked up. At the top of the doorway three small webs were being constructed. On each web, working busily was one of Charlotte's daughters.

Can I take this to mean, asked Wilbur, that you have definitely decided to live here in the barn cellar, and that I am going to have *three* friends?

You can indeed, said the spiders.

What are your names, please? asked Wilbur, trembling with joy.

## **Multiple Choice:** Circle the letter of the BEST answer.

1. How does Fern pamper Wilbur? **Both** must be true!
   a. She takes him for rides and lets him wade in the mud.
   b. She gives him candy and lets him wade in the water.
   c. She takes him for rides and lets him sleep in her bed.

2. What does Charlotte do that Wilbur describes as "real thoughtful"?
   a. She gives her prey an anaesthetic before drinking their blood.
   b. She becomes his friend.
   c. She captures flies so they won't bother other animals.

3. What bad news is spreading in the barnyard?
   a. Wilbur is going to be killed at Christmastime.
   b. Templeton has captured a baby goose.
   c. Fern can't visit Wilbur anymore.

4. On what attribute does Charlotte rely to help her solve problems?
   a. She relies on her willingness to work hard.
   b. She depends on her intelligence; her ability to think of good ideas.
   c. She depends on her ability to wait patiently.

5. How is Templeton convinced to get words from the dump?
   a. Templeton is finally convinced that it won't take much extra time or effort since he makes regular trips to the dump anyway.
   b. The old sheep points out that saving Wilbur means he will always have leftover food to eat.
   c. The goose offers him another "dud" egg in the future if he will help Wilbur now.

6. Why does Charlotte say she cannot go to the fair with Wilbur?
   a. Nature says it is time to lay her eggs and she cannot delay it, not even for Wilbur.
   b. She is confident her plan is working well and Wilbur no longer needs her help.
   c. She wants Wilbur to gain confidence by going alone and succeeding without further help.

7. What advice does the old sheep give Wilbur before he is crated for the fair?
   a. He tells Wilbur to be sure to eat plenty of food before leaving because he may not get fed again until late in the evening.
   b. He tells Wilbur to struggle as the men try to put him into the crate.
   c. He tells Wilbur to watch Charlotte carefully since she is so weak.

8. What changes does Charlotte begin to notice in herself while at the fair?
   a. She feels a lack of energy and is tired all the time.
   b. She suddenly feels tired and hungry all the time.
   c. She becomes very hungry and anxious to make a new web.

9. What is Wilbur's response to Templeton's pronouncement of Uncle's prize and Wilbur's death?
   a. Wilbur panics and yells that he does not want to die.
   b. Wilbur remains fairly calm and changes the subject.
   c. Wilbur starts to cry and asks Charlotte to tell him what to do.

10. Why is Wilbur so sad several days after Charlotte's children are born?
   a. He misses Charlotte and wants to share the excitement of their birth with her.
   b. The baby spiders make web balloons and float away to find new homes.
   c. He is lonely and bored because Fern no longer comes to visit.

## Character, Setting, Plot: Write a short phrase or sentence to answer each question.

1. What does the term "character" mean?______________________________

______________________________

2. Who are the two main characters in *Charlotte's Web*? ______________________________

______________________________

3. Describe the setting of *Charlotte's Web.* ______________________________

______________________________

______________________________

4. Tell what the term "plot" means in literature.______________________________

______________________________

______________________________

5. What is the **overall** plot of *Charlotte's Web*? What is the one central problem in the book and how is it solved? ______________________________

______________________________

______________________________

______________________________

______________________________

______________________________

## **Short Answer:** Write a phrase or sentence for each question.

1. What does the word "arable" mean? Why is it a good name for a farm family? ________________

2. Choose one minor character from the book (Mrs. Zuckerman, Dr. Dorian, Lurvy) and describe this person's reaction to Charlotte's web. ________________

3. List three ways in which life on the Zuckerman farm changes as a result of Wilbur's fame. ________

4. Name one specific action Templeton does to help Wilbur and describe how it displays his selfishness. ________________

5. Describe one specific character quality that Wilbur learns from Charlotte and later displays toward her children. ________________

## **Paragraph:** 3-5 sentences

In your own words write a paragraph describing your favorite character from *Charlotte's Web*. Include details about the character's appearance and personality. Also explain why you like this character.

# Quizzes & Final Test Key

# Charlotte's Web Quiz 1
Chapters 1-7

Name ______________________________

Date ______________________________

Write the letter of the vocabulary word on the line in front of its definition.

| | | |
|---|---|---|
| 1. d | state of being held against your will | a. runt |
| 2. i | constant; neverending | b. injustice |
| 3. b | unfairness | c. gaze |
| 4. f | one who habitually overeats | d. captivity |
| 5. j | strongly disliked | e. commotion |
| 6. g | to bear, tolerate | f. glutton |
| 7. a | smallest of the litter | g. endure |
| 8. e | noisy, confused activity | h. blundered |
| 9. h | moved carelessly | i. unremitting |
| 10. c | to look at steadily | j. loathed |

Match each name below with a character description.

| | | | | |
|---|---|---|---|---|
| **Mr. Arable** | **Mr. Zuckerman** | **goose** | **Wilbur** | **Charlotte** |
| **Lurvy** | **Templeton** | **Fern** | **old sheep** | **lamb** |

1. Mr. Arable — only distributed pigs to early risers
2. Wilbur — thought he was too young for freedom
3. Templeton — a glutton, but not a merrymaker
4. lamb — believed that pigs were less than nothing
5. Lurvy — first noticed something was wrong with the pig
6. Charlotte — thoughtfully gave her victims an anaesthetic
7. Fern — was treated as an equal by the animals in the barn
8. Mr. Zuckerman — bought Wilbur for $6.00
9. old sheep — spread the bad news about the conspiracy on the farm
10. goose — advised Wilbur during his escape

Choose the **best** answer for each question.

1. What is the first thing Fern teaches Wilbur?
   - (a.) to take milk from a bottle
   - b. to sleep in a baby carriage
   - c. to follow her around the farm

2. How does Fern pamper Wilbur? **Both** must be true!
   - a. She takes him for rides and lets him sleep in her bed.
   - (b.) She takes him for rides and lets him wade in the mud.
   - c. She gives him candy and lets him wade in the water.

3. Who is the first animal Wilbur meets?
   - a. Templeton
   - b. Charlotte
   - (c.) the goose

4. Why does Wilbur so willingly follow the advice of the goose at first?
   - a. He is curious and adventurous.
   - b. He wants to visit Fern.
   - (c.) He is bored and discouraged.

5. What is Wilbur's pleasant surprise at the end of the rainy day?
   - a. Fern visits unexpectedly.
   - (b.) He hears a voice offering him friendship.
   - c. Lurvy brings him extra slops.

6. How does the author describe Charlotte?
   - (a.) She is a large, gray spider, about the size of a gumdrop.
   - b. She is a large, black spider, about the size of a penny.
   - c. She is a large, brown spider, about the size of a grape.

7. What word does Charlotte use to greet Wilbur for the first time?
   - a. "Hello!"
   - b. "Greetings!"
   - (c.) "Salutations!"

8. Where does Templeton put the "dud" goose egg?
   a. He rolls it to the dump.
   (b.) He rolls it to his lair under the trough.
   c. He rolls it to his lair under the farmhouse.

9. What does Charlotte do that Wilbur describes as "real thoughtful"?
   (a.) She gives her prey an anaesthetic before drinking their blood.
   b. She captures flies so they won't bother other animals.
   c. She becomes his friend.

10. What bad news is spreading in the barnyard?
   a. Templeton has captured a baby goose.
   (b.) Wilbur is going to be killed at Christmastime.
   c. Fern can't visit Wilbur anymore.

Answer the following questions in complete sentences.

1. What does the word "arable" mean? Why is it a good name for a farm family?

   "Arable" means land suitable for farming. It is a good name because the Arables are farmers.

2. What reasons did Father give for insisting that Fern sell Wilbur?

   Wilbur was beginning to eat more food. Mr. Arable was not willing to provide food for him any longer because the cost of the food would be more than the price he could get selling him later. Mr. Arable had already sold Wilbur's siblings.

3. What important event, announced by Charlotte, happened in the barn cellar?

   Charlotte made the announcement that the goslings had hatched.

4. Explain Wilbur's statement "…what a gamble friendship is!"

   When you first befriend someone, you don't really know them well and the friendship may or may not work out. You need to be willing to get to know the other person instead of dismissing them because you have differences.

5. What promise does Charlotte make to Wilbur?

   Charlotte promises to save Wilbur from death.

# Charlotte's Web Quiz 2
Chapters 8-15

Name ______________________

Date ______________________

Write the letter of the vocabulary word on the line in front of its definition.

| | | |
|---|---|---|
| 1. g | pleased; satisfied | a. principal |
| 2. c | gathering; calling up | b. writhing |
| 3. i | easily deceived | c. summoning |
| 4. e | unfriendly; bad-tempered | d. versatile |
| 5. a | main; primary | e. surly |
| 6. h | trembled | f. sternly |
| 7. b | squirming | g. gratified |
| 8. f | seriously; firmly | h. quivered |
| 9. j | endless; continuous | i. gullible |
| 10. d | adaptable; can adjust easily | j. incessant |

Match each name below with a character description.

| | | | | |
|---|---|---|---|---|
| **Avery** | **Templeton** | **Fern** | **Mrs. Arable** | **Charlotte** |
| **Dr. Dorian** | **Mrs. Zuckerman** | **Wilbur** | **old sheep** | **Lurvy** |

1. Mrs. Zuckerman — believed that the spider was extraordinary, not the pig
2. Lurvy — built a crate for Wilbur
3. Templeton — found the words "With New Radiant Action" at the dump
4. Fern — was impressed with the stories of Charlotte's cousins
5. Wilbur — worked hard to make a web, but failed
6. Mrs. Arable — worried about Fern's claim to understand animals
7. Avery — tried to capture Charlotte, but failed
8. old sheep — convinced Templeton to get new words from the dump
9. Charlotte — believed that people are very gullible
10. Dr. Dorian — thought if people talked less, animals might talk more

1. How does Wilbur try to imitate Charlotte?
   a. He offers friendship to a baby goose.
   b. He catches some flies and eats them.
   (c.) He tries to spin a web of his own.

2. Why does Charlotte think her webs are better than human "webs"?
   a. Her webs are more easily changed and therefore more creative.
   (b.) Her webs are built faster and are more practical.
   c. Her webs are more beautiful to look at.

3. On what attribute does Charlotte rely to help her solve problems?
   (a.) She depends on her ability to wait patiently.
   b. She relies on her willingness to work hard.
   c. She depends on her intelligence; her ability to think of good ideas.

4. What catastrophe is prevented from happening in the barn cellar?
   (a.) Charlotte gets caught by Avery.
   b. The baby geese get loose in the barnyard.
   c. Fern is no longer allowed to visit Wilbur.

5. Who is the first person to discover the "miracle" web?
   a. Mr. Zuckerman
   (b.) Lurvy
   c. Fern

6. How is Mrs. Zuckerman's view of the "miracle" web different from everyone else's view of it?
   (a.) She thinks the spider is special, not necessarily the pig.
   b. She is busy and doesn't take much interest in the web at all.
   c. She becomes very excited and plans to buy a deep freeze when they are famous.

7. How is Templeton convinced to get words from the dump?
   a. The goose offers him another "dud" egg in the future if he will help Wilbur now.
   b. Templeton is finally convinced that it won't take much extra time or effort since he makes regular trips to the dump anyway.
   (c.) The old sheep points out that saving Wilbur means he will always have his leftover food to eat.

8. How does Charlotte entertain herself while weaving?

    (a.) She talks to herself and cheers herself on as she weaves.
    b. She tells the other animals stories about her amazing cousins.
    c. She sings songs to Wilbur.

9. What does Dr. Dorian think about Fern's love of animals and spending so much time in the barn?

    a. He thinks it is dangerous, but he's not worried because she will soon grow out of it.
    (b.) He believes her love for animals is healthy and therefore is not worried about her.
    c. He agrees with Mrs. Arable that Fern should not be allowed to spend much time in the barn.

10. Why does Charlotte say she cannot go to the fair with Wilbur?

    (a.) Nature says it is time to lay her eggs and she cannot delay it, not even for Wilbur.
    b. She wants Wilbur to gain confidence by going alone and succeeding without further help.
    c. She is confident her plan is working well and Wilbur no longer needs her help.

Answer the following questions in complete sentences.

1. What plan does Charlotte come up with to save Wilbur's life? Why does she think it will work?

    Charlotte plans to play a trick on Zuckerman because people are not as smart as insects. They are gullible.

2. Name two specific ways in which the webs affect life on the Zuckerman farm.

    Possible answers: people come to see Wilbur and the web, Mr. Zuckerman neglects his farm work and wears good clothes, Mrs. Zuckerman prepares special meals for Wilbur, Lurvy shaves and gets a haircut.

3. What is Wilbur's reaction to the second word in the web ("terrific")? What does this show about his character? Wilbur blushes and says he is just an average pig. This reaction shows that he is humble.

4. As summer comes to an end, what are Wilbur and Charlotte each looking forward to?

    Wilbur is looking forward to the fair, and Charlotte is looking forward to laying her eggs. They conflict because Wilbur wants Charlotte with him at the fair, but she needs to stay on the farm.

5. Choose one of the following characters and describe how they show friendship towards Wilbur. (Fern, the goose, the old sheep) **Charlotte** stands up for Wilbur, and she sacrifices her time and energy to help him. **Fern** saves Wilbur's life and visits him. **The goose** is friendly and kind and tries to suggest words. **The old sheep** tells him the truth and convinces Templeton to help.

# Charlotte's Web Quiz 3
Chapters 16-22

Name ______________________

Date ______________________

Write the letter of the vocabulary word on the line in front of its definition.

| | | | |
|---|---|---|---|
| 1. d | to exceed; go beyond | a. | listless |
| 2. g | to move upward | b. | gorge |
| 3. a | tired, no energy | c. | sentiments |
| 4. j | sharp; highly developed | d. | surpass |
| 5. e | greatest work | e. | masterpiece |
| 6. b | a binge of overeating | f. | desolation |
| 7. i | to restore to consciousness | g. | ascend |
| 8. c | statements based on emotions | h. | retorted |
| 9. f | loneliness | i. | revive |
| 10. h | replied | j. | keen |

Match each name below with a character description.

| | | | | |
|---|---|---|---|---|
| **Uncle** | **Mrs. Zuckerman** | **Avery** | **old sheep** | **Charlotte** |
| **Wilbur** | **Aranea** | **geese** | **Lurvy** | **Templeton** |

1. Uncle — won a first prize blue ribbon at the fair
2. Lurvy — won an Indian blanket
3. old sheep — convinced Templeton that the fair is a rat's paradise
4. Wilbur — fainted from all the attention
5. Templeton — gorged himself at the fair
6. Aranea — one of Charlotte's baby spiders
7. Avery — loved lots of attention and performed to get more of it
8. Mrs. Zuckerman — gave Wilbur a buttermilk bath
9. geese — cheered
10. Charlotte — created her *magnum opus*

Choose the **best** answer for each question.

1. What special treatment does Wilbur get before departing for the fair?
   a. Wilbur receives extra slops in his trough.
   (b.) Wilbur gets a buttermilk bath.
   c. Wilbur is petted and very carefully lifted and placed into the crate.

2. What advice does the old sheep give Wilbur before he is crated for the fair?
   (a.) He tells Wilbur to struggle as the men try to put him into the crate.
   b. He tells Wilbur to be sure to eat plenty of food before leaving because he may not get fed again until late in the evening.
   c. He tells Wilbur to watch Charlotte carefully since she is so weak.

3. Why does Charlotte dislike Uncle?
   a. Charlotte sees how large he is and is concerned that he may win the prize.
   b. Charlotte dislikes Uncle because he tells weak jokes and has an unusual name.
   (c.) Charlotte thinks he is dirty, unpleasant in personality, and he tells weak jokes.

4. What changes does Charlotte begin to notice in herself while at the fair?
   (a.) She feels a lack of energy and is tired all the time.
   b. She becomes very hungry and anxious to make a new web.
   c. She suddenly feels tired and hungry all the time.

5. What does Charlotte do at the fair that is unusual? **Both** must be true!
   a. Charlotte leaves her web to hunt for flies in another corner of the barn.
   (b.) Charlotte refuses to sing Wilbur a song and she leaves her web.
   c. Charlotte tells Uncle stories about her cousins and makes something for herself.

6. What is Wilbur's response to Templeton's pronouncement of Uncle's prize and Wilbur's resulting death?
   a. Wilbur panics and yells that he does not want to die.
   b. Wilbur starts to cry and asks Charlotte to tell him what to do.
   (c.) Wilbur remains fairly calm and changes the subject.

7. What does Fern prefer to do rather than watch the award ceremony?
   a. Fern prefers to spend time and money in the midway.
   b. Fern prefers to sit quietly in the barn watching Charlotte.
   (c.) Fern prefers to ride the Ferris wheel with Henry Fussy.

8. How does Wilbur react to all the attention he receives when he gets his special award?
   - (a.) He faints, but he enjoys all the attention.
   - b. He hates all the attention because he is shy and modest.
   - c. He loves all the attention and acts silly to make the people laugh.

9. How does Wilbur transport the egg sac?
   - a. Wilbur rolls it carefully into his crate and buries it in the soft straw.
   - (b.) Wilbur carries it in his mouth because he knows it is water proof.
   - c. Wilbur makes a deal with Templeton to carry it since he doesn't have hands or paws.

10. Why is Wilbur so sad several days after Charlotte's children are born?
   - a. He is lonely and bored because Fern no longer comes to visit.
   - b. He misses Charlotte and wants to share the excitement of their birth with her.
   - (c.) The baby spiders make web balloons and float away to find new homes.

Answer the following questions in complete sentences.

1. What is the last word Charlotte weaves into her web, and why is it a perfect choice?

   The last word is "humble." It is the perfect choice because it means "near the ground" and "not proud"; Wilbur is both.

2. Describe Charlotte's egg sac. Why does she call it her *magnum opus*?

   The egg sac looks like a cocoon; it is peach-colored and looks like cotton candy. It is her masterpiece, the greatest thing she has ever made.

3. How do Charlotte and Wilbur spend their last moments together?

   They acknowledge their friendship. Wilbur says that Charlotte saved his life and pledges his willingness to give his life for her. Wilbur winks at Charlotte with her egg sac safely in his mouth.

4. How does Wilbur prepare for the birth of Charlotte's children?

   He places the egg sac close to himself in the warm manure. He warms it with his breath on cold nights. Then, he waits patiently for them to hatch.

5. Describe two changes that have occurred in Wilbur since the beginning of the book.

   Possible answers: He has learned the true meaning of friendship, he has learned not to make judgments about others, he has learned to accept others as they are and to appreciate them, he has learned selflessness, contentment, and how to get along with difficult people.

# Charlotte's Web Final Test

Name ______________________

Date ______________________

## Vocabulary: Write the letter of the vocabulary word next to its definition.

1. __e__ to look at steadily
2. __g__ to restore to consciousness
3. __j__ easily deceived
4. __f__ endless; continuous
5. __d__ adaptable; can adjust easily
6. __h__ one who habitually overeats
7. __c__ trembled
8. __i__ statements based on emotions
9. __b__ gathering; calling up
10. __a__ tired; no energy

a. listless
b. summoning
c. quivered
d. versatile
e. gaze
f. incessant
g. revived
h. glutton
i. sentiments
j. gullible

## Character Identification: Choose the name that matches each description and write it on the line.

| Fern | Templeton | Lurvy | Mrs. Arable | Wilbur |
|---|---|---|---|---|
| Dr. Dorian | Mrs. Zuckerman | goose | Charlotte | old sheep |

1. __goose__ advised Wilbur during his escape
2. __Templeton__ a glutton, but not a merrymaker
3. __Lurvy__ won an Indian blanket
4. __Charlotte__ believed that people are very gullible
5. __Fern__ was treated as an equal by the animals in the barn
6. __old sheep__ convinced Templeton to go to the dump and the fair
7. __Mrs. Arable__ worried about Fern's claim to understand animals
8. __Dr. Dorian__ thought if people talked less, animals might talk more
9. __Wilbur__ worked hard to make a web, but failed
10. __Mrs. Zuckerman__ believed that the spider was extraordinary, not the pig

## **Who Said That?:** Match each name to a quotation below and write the name on the line.

| Wilbur | Templeton | Fern | Charlotte | Uncle |
|---|---|---|---|---|
| lamb | Mr. Zuckerman | Mr. Arable | old sheep | goose |

1. Charlotte "Stop your crying! I can't stand hysterics."
2. Wilbur "I think I'm going to faint."
3. Mr. Zuckerman "Humble, now isn't that just the word for Wilbur."
4. Fern "But it's unfair ... The pig couldn't help being born small, could it?"
5. old sheep "they're fattening you up because they're going to kill you"
6. lamb "Pigs mean less than nothing to me."
7. Mr. Arable "I only distribute pigs to early risers."
8. Uncle "What did you think I was, a spring chicken?"
9. goose "No-no-no ... It's the old pail trick, Wilbur. Don't fall for it!"
10. Templeton "I must have eaten the remains of thirty lunches."

## **Dialogue:** Add quotation marks in the following paragraphs where they are needed.

"Salutations!" it said. "I'm up here."

"So am I," said another tiny voice.

"So am I," said a third voice. "Three of us are staying. We like this place, and we like *you*."

Wilbur looked up. At the top of the doorway three small webs were being constructed. On each web, working busily was one of Charlotte's daughters.

"Can I take this to mean," asked Wilbur, "that you have definitely decided to live here in the barn cellar, and that I am going to have *three* friends?"

"You can indeed," said the spiders.

"What are your names, please?" asked Wilbur, trembling with joy.

## **Multiple Choice:** Circle the letter of the BEST answer.

1. How does Fern pamper Wilbur? **Both** must be true!
   - (a.) She takes him for rides and lets him wade in the mud.
   - b. She gives him candy and lets him wade in the water.
   - c. She takes him for rides and lets him sleep in her bed.

2. What does Charlotte do that Wilbur describes as "real thoughtful"?
   - (a.) She gives her prey an anaesthetic before drinking their blood.
   - b. She becomes his friend.
   - c. She captures flies so they won't bother other animals.

3. What bad news is spreading in the barnyard?
   - (a.) Wilbur is going to be killed at Christmastime.
   - b. Templeton has captured a baby goose.
   - c. Fern can't visit Wilbur anymore.

4. On what attribute does Charlotte rely to help her solve problems?
   - a. She relies on her willingness to work hard.
   - b. She depends on her intelligence; her ability to think of good ideas.
   - (c.) She depends on her ability to wait patiently.

5. How is Templeton convinced to get words from the dump?
   - a. Templeton is finally convinced that it won't take much extra time or effort since he makes regular trips to the dump anyway.
   - (b.) The old sheep points out that saving Wilbur means he will always have leftover food to eat.
   - c. The goose offers him another "dud" egg in the future if he will help Wilbur now.

6. Why does Charlotte say she cannot go to the fair with Wilbur?
   - (a.) Nature says it is time to lay her eggs and she cannot delay it, not even for Wilbur.
   - b. She is confident her plan is working well and Wilbur no longer needs her help.
   - c. She wants Wilbur to gain confidence by going alone and succeeding without further help.

7. What advice does the old sheep give Wilbur before he is crated for the fair?
   - a. He tells Wilbur to be sure to eat plenty of food before leaving because he may not get fed again until late in the evening.
   - (b.) He tells Wilbur to struggle as the men try to put him into the crate.
   - c. He tells Wilbur to watch Charlotte carefully since she is so weak.

8. What changes does Charlotte begin to notice in herself while at the fair?
   (a.) She feels a lack of energy and is tired all the time.
   b. She suddenly feels tired and hungry all the time.
   c. She becomes very hungry and anxious to make a new web.

9. What is Wilbur's response to Templeton's pronouncement of Uncle's prize and Wilbur's death?
   a. Wilbur panics and yells that he does not want to die.
   (b.) Wilbur remains fairly calm and changes the subject.
   c. Wilbur starts to cry and asks Charlotte to tell him what to do.

10. Why is Wilbur so sad several days after Charlotte's children are born?
   a. He misses Charlotte and wants to share the excitement of their birth with her.
   (b.) The baby spiders make web balloons and float away to find new homes.
   c. He is lonely and bored because Fern no longer comes to visit.

## Character, Setting, Plot: Write a short phrase or sentence to answer each question.

1. What does the term "character" mean? ____

   Character means who is in the story.

2. Who are the two main characters in *Charlotte's Web*? ____

   The main characters are Wilbur the pig and Charlotte the spider.

3. Describe the setting of *Charlotte's Web.* ____

   The book takes place primarily on the Zuckerman farm and at the county fair, sometime in the past.

4. Tell what the term "plot" means in literature. ____

   Plot means action or what happens in the story.

5. What is the **overall** plot of *Charlotte's Web*? What is the one central problem in the book and how is it solved? ____

   When a young runt pig is born, Fern rescues it from death, raises it, and sells it to her uncle. It soon becomes clear that Wilbur is merely being raised in order to be killed later at Christmastime. Wilbur's new friend, Charlotte, a spider, promises to save his life. She does this by weaving words that describe Wilbur into her web, causing people to see him differently, value him more, and decide not to kill him.

## **Short Answer:** Write a phrase or sentence for each question.

1. What does the word "arable" mean? Why is it a good name for a farm family?

   "Arable" means land suitable for farming. It is a good name because the Arables are farmers.

2. Choose one minor character from the book (Mrs. Zuckerman, Dr. Dorian, Lurvy) and describe this person's reaction to Charlotte's web. Mrs. Zuckerman suspects the spider is special, not the pig; Lurvy is awestruck and kneels down to say a prayer; Dr. Dorian thinks any spider web is a miracle since they do it from instinct, not needing to be taught.

3. List three ways in which life on the Zuckerman farm changes as a result of Wilbur's fame.

   Possible answers: people come to see Wilbur and the web, farm work is neglected, the Zuckermans and Lurvy dress up, Wilbur is fed more food and given clean straw.

4. Name one specific action Templeton does to help Wilbur and describe how it displays his selfishness. Possible answers: He gets words from the dump so he has Wilbur's leftovers to eat, he goes to the fair for all the promised food, he bites Wilbur's tail so Wilbur lives and he will continue to be fed, he rescues the egg sac after Wilbur promises he can eat first from his trough.

5. Describe one specific character quality that Wilbur learns from Charlotte and later displays toward her children. He offers to help them however he can. He thinks of their needs ahead of his own and makes them a priority. He offers his friendship to them before he knows them well.

## **Paragraph:** 3-5 sentences

In your own words write a paragraph describing your favorite character from *Charlotte's Web*. Include details about the character's appearance and personality. Also explain why you like this character.

Answers will vary.